Financial Freedom

THE CHOICE

Edited by
JUDI POPE KOTEEN

Published by
Beyond Words Publishing, Inc.
Pumpkin Ridge Road
Route 3, Box 492-B
Hillsboro, OR 97123
Phone: 503-647-5109
Toll Free: 1-800-284-9673

DISCLAIMER
This book is designed to provide information in regard to the subject matter covered. The purpose of this book is to educate and entertain. The author, editors, and publisher shall have neither liability nor responsibility to any person or entity with respect to any loss or damage caused, directly or indirectly, by the information contained in this book.

Printed in the United States of America
by Arcata Graphics, Kingsport, Tennessee

Library of Congress Catalog Card Number: 90-080959
ISBN: 0-941831-16-7

Special thanks to Adrianne and Jennifer,
I love you, my little lights; to my mother, who taught me
impeccability; and to Earl, who is on the greatest search of all.

To all who desire to be free

Dedication and Thanks

I am grateful to Bernie for making me stay up late and talk. To Minnie for pushing me. To Maureen for loving me, believing in me, and supporting me. To Stan for healing all of us and for making me question. To Mary for introducing me to the wind. To the Carols and Jeffrey and Tom and Pavel and David for your laughter and your tears. To Scott for loving himself. To Joe for keeping me on line and not in line. To Marri for not being silent. To JZ for allowing me. To Richard and Cindy for asking me.

Foreword

In 1977, Ramtha appeared before JZ Knight in the doorway of her kitchen in Tacoma, Washington. Nothing has been the same since.

Ramtha is an enigma. He calls himself such. And without a doubt, as the focus of society moves beyond the phenomenon of channeling and more people begin to take a serious look at the message, Ramtha will be hailed as one of the greatest communicators and teachers of all time.

He lived on earth 35,000 years ago and for the better part of that life was a savage conqueror, until he was wounded in a battle. He withdrew to a mountain to contemplate life and spent seven years upon a barren rock, considering the sun and moon, and life and death, and things that never seem to change. And when he left that rock and returned to his waiting army, he returned an enlightened being, for he had seen through the illusion called life. He stayed and taught his people for many years and ultimately ascended before thousands. He is "The Ram" around which the Hindu people built their religion.

He describes himself as part of a brotherhood of beings who love humankind greatly, who have come with information to help us make the choices necessary in order for us to gain personal sovereignty in the days to come. His is an enabling message, an empowering message.

Once, when asked what he would say if he could reach the whole world with a single most important message, he said, "I would tell you that you are God and that you are greatly loved."

Books created from Ramtha's words are based on weekend events called Intensives, where he speaks extemporaneously about a given subject.

The Intensive this book was based on was delivered in March, 1987. Attendees followed the directions given for the process of manifesting experientially. Intensives are a process. A flow begins with an initial delivered understanding, so that everyone begins from the same point of reference, the same premise. The teaching moves along an emotional pathway, with some information delivered in a straightforward manner and some of it in pure poetry.

This particular Intensive was more participatory than most, as dictated by the subject matter. If your life is your creation, then certainly your manifestations are also. There are times in this book where you are directed to sit on the floor, or ideally the ground. It is recommended that you stay with the process at those times and work!

The toasts are done with lemon water and the prayers are repeated out loud to align and to honor the Father.

Table of Contents

Special Acknowledgment

I am extremely grateful to author Stephen Smoke and to Beyond Words Publishing, Inc. for allowing the wonderful lines from their transformative book, *Trick of the Light*, to be used liberally here.

"But one thing I'm finding out is that there is no such thing as an accident."

Trick of the Light

THE CHOICE

*"Your ad in the Yellow Pages says you
can find **anyone**."*
*She paused, took another puff, exhaled,
then said slowly, "I want you to find God."*

Trick of the Light

The Epic Journey of Man

So you want money.

I once asked a room full of people what they wanted. And they said, "To be God. And to be rich."

So let's get right down to it. You want money; I call it gold. But we should get clear on that point straight away. Your government doesn't call money gold anymore, not since the Sixteenth Amendment to your Constitution allowed income tax to come into being and the Federal Reserve system was formulated by international bankers.

I'll bet you think because it says "Federal"
Reserve that it's owned by your government.

Well, it doesn't and it isn't. The Federal Reserve is owned by very powerful people who for eons, through religious dogma, have created war to gain power. Those are the same people who no longer back your dollars in gold, because your country does not have enough gold to back up the paper. And it is these sovereign individuals that control your world government. They dictate how much and how little your paper is worth. It is not you who create inflation and deflation; it is not you who create rises in stocks and bonds! That is done by the ones who control the world through money.

So I prefer gold over and above your dollars, because in the twinkling of an eye, your paper can be worthless. And gold, which is a tender, soft, shining, wondrous metal, whose rarity and beauty has adorned kings and noblemen, and the rich, and sometimes even the poor, has always had its value.

Gold is a sensitive metal. It is given in love and affection because it is soft. Soft metal absorbs the emotional frequencies that lie outside of the body physical. Your gold has had an emotional value forever. Put on the breastplate of a king and within moments you will feel the glory, because his emotion, his glory, his pre-eminence of attitude in wearing it, is locked into the metal.

If you see a mask of a long dead Pharaoh, look deeply into the black and hollow eyes and the finely chiseled nose, and you will feel the tragedy and know the majesty, because the carved gold face emanates the whole of the wearer.

So, gold has held value for so long because it is bright, yellow, and beautiful? No. Because it has emotional impact. Gold is an unprejudiced metal. It does not determine hate, or lust for power, or love and passion, or betrayal. It simply holds the emotion. In other words, gold is the soul of all metals.

Rather than give credence to this fallible illusion of your paper economics, I will talk about your quest for financial independence in terms of gold. For when you have gold in your hands, you become immortal with that energy.

By the way, the greatest gold you can get has been melted down and blocked, and owned by no one. Then you can implant power and an emotional reaction to the metal.

But let's go back to your government for a moment, for you are in a most precarious position regarding these matters.

You have been blatantly ignorant about where your money comes from.

Does it occur to you that one day your dollar might not be valuable, no matter how much you have in your treasury? Does it occur to you that there are people in high places that control the world's power?

You are fallible because you have been in **need** and **ignorance**. You can hoard great sums of paper in a bank, but if the paper has no value, what will you eat? The paper?

You have closed down your awareness regarding possibilities. If all you want is money, you will surely die unhappy. I assure you of that. For money will mean nothing when the spirit calls the soul from the body, and you pass this time and place, this world controlled through mathematical equations. It will mean nothing!

But that is where your quest has been. You are very holy people except when money is involved.

The rascals who have led you as a nation and enslaved you through belief have continually said you are born wicked in your soul from birth. Well, you are not. You just **need**. You are born divine. The greatest legacy I will leave you for all time has never changed. Whether or not I put my consonants in the wrong positions and my verbs at the beginning and my nouns at the end, the message is clear.

You and the Father are one. And the life that you lead, that you breathe, that you permeate with your existence, is his love called grace. The kingdom of heaven is within you. Not in your castles. Not in your gold, your money, your ignorance. It is **in you**.

And you say to me, "That is nothing new. Big deal."

Of course that's not new to you. But precious few of you have ever lived it. Listen. It's new when you embrace it completely and your fickle mind opens up and allows the power within. That is my greatest legacy that transcends everything that you have in your bank account and everything you wish you had there. When you seek to embrace the kingdom within impeccably and above everything else, and you live that truth in the midst of fire, then everything else comes into focus.

This is where you say, "But I still need help and I don't think I can do it by myself."

I know many of you are crippled. You have always been crippled. You are the godless who have always been dead because you have never lived. You are godless because you have never known the God within, and you have never lived because you aren't really living if you don't know the God within.

You have simply been scrambling in your ignorance to survive. You have been trying to keep your head above fear and threats and intimidation. You have been trying to buy yourself out of whatever mess you're in. But you'll never get beyond it that way because you have never truly **lived**. When you are godless, you can only survive by clawing, scraping, biting, pecking, despising, gossiping, envying, and maliciously destroying everything that reflects what you lack. That is not living.

The rich man lives in a tower with gilded walls and Persian rugs and golden plates. His rooms smell of lavender and rose water, and spice and jasmine flow from his fountain while he dines on pheasant, and fish, and figs, and fruits and all sorts of wondrous things. And he sits there and he is still unhappy.

And then there is the man who has none of these things. Stale bread and water and a sweet meat are a celebration to him on special days. He has only a rough linen on his back and hardly ever a bed to sleep in, and yet there is joy. And when he walks by the palace, he does not envy or despise the rich man, but loves him as an equal. And he finds his days not a dreadful experience of survival, but an opportunity to be a ray of light, embracing, encompassing, loving, being free and **alive**.

I can reverse the characters and have the poor man be envious, despicable, a malicious gossiper, and the rich man can wake up in joy, and it would still be by the **emotion** that he is alive. **Aliveness** and **joy** are not the result of what you own in the material sense.

The legacy that I have taught you for the past decade has not changed. For that is the zenith of a life that wakes up from a requiem of sleep into a mass of understanding.

When you own what's inside you, it doesn't matter what's outside you.

When I consider what you are going for, in asking for financial freedom, I see you as brave, courageous, and very admirable. Why do I say that? Because everyone else has rebuked you for desiring gold and somehow they have attempted to fit that rebuke into what they call God's plan.

This controversy about gold and God is the same ignorance that has kept you from embracing your legacy. Is God exempt from the wickedness of man and his peril with money?

All is God. How can you say that gold does not exist. How can you say that it is not synonymous with life. Gold is only the conduit of emotion. And it is an exchange of that emotional energy that is the investment that allows you to go further.

Wake up! Those that rule your world, rule it through money because money is power. A wealthy man is a powerful man, and he desires wealth because it gives him power. Power is what he seeks and religion has been the pawn on the board. And the churches have been among the wealthiest in the world.

Every war has been fought over religious belief. Which God is going to win?

The people you call Irish were called Norsemen in my day. That was when the sun broke through and the ice was retreating. The Irish are slaughtering humans and justifying it because it is a war of religious belief. But it is the power behind the religious belief that has set it all up to break down the system, to gain control.

If you understand the dark side of gold, you can understand the light that brings out the shadows. Gold, power, and religion have been a wicked combination throughout your history, because every religious belief is tainted in the blood of those that they conquered in order to become established.

And the gold they have acquired lies in vaults. But God, which is life, which is intelligence, forever and ever and ever, is the life that has created the gold. It is coagulated thought of God. Just as your dollars are. Just as you are. There is no difference.

Ignorance has suppressed man into a groveling state of dependence and need. And somewhere in there, you have drawn a fine line between God that is spiritual and gold that is money. Some of you actually think there is some sort of demarcation between gold and God. And if you are among those who think that way, you are not only a hypocrite, but you are cutting your own throat, for the powerful are hoarding the gold in the name of God.

And the hypocritical politician who says that man is wicked if he seeks gold but divine is he seeks God is lusting for the gold to give him power to rule the ignorant!

None of this is wrong; it is simply how you have set it up to be. But the one who condemns gold, condemns God. For where does gold come from? What is it made of? What gives it life? It isn't even the gold itself, but the **attitude** behind gold that has made it valuable. Gold is not wrong. All you have to do is look around you and realize that everything came from God, and the only one who is in control of that reality is the Father within you.

If all life is God, then so is your gold.

And what's wrong with that? You have made it wrong through **limited thinking and the attitude behind that thinking.** And that is what we will address in this book. You've already heard, "You are God," and, "The Father is within." But it hasn't done anything for you yet, because you still have your hand out asking, wanting, needing. You are unhappy because you don't have enough.

When do you have enough to be filled inside? You never do.

You are to be admired for addressing this subject and continuing to read. It says a lot about your courage, your selfishness, and your needs. And if you don't comprehend the greatest legacy of all, and you simply **want**, it is still alright.

Sooner or later you will realize the greatest need—to know God. The greatest need is to embrace God, to live God; until you see that **need** is a limitation and the freedom to exist in harmony with all life comes from within.

A master in the last days before Christhood leaves no tracks. But for now, with as much gold as you wear around your neck and carry in your purses and wallets, your tracks are very indented.

It is important that you reason what I am saying, Everything that I am saying, if you reason it, will fulfill a dream that you have. Because knowledge, not ritual, is enlightenment, and enlightenment means to be **in knowledge of.**

How do you know truth?
When it rattles your boxes.

When you despise me one moment for something I said that was painfully true, and love me the next moment because you read something that exalted you, and you wanted it to be true.

That is how you know truth.
You react to it.

Some of you have heard for years that God the Father and the Kingdom are within, but you still don't get it. And that is alright, too. Because sooner or later, you are going to get there.

I will give you a very simple and profound truth.

A dream unrealized is a limitation to Christhood.

Consider yourself. You have all of these illusions, these dreams of things you want to do and have. You want to feel important. You want to feel secure. You want to feel wonderful. Your wish list ranges from wanting to have your face lifted to owning all of your land and the house of your dreams. You want four years of food and the children's education paid for. You want everything you can possibly think of stored away, so you can sit back, have your biscuits and jam, pick your teeth, watch the sun go down, and say, "hallelujah."

All of those things are layers of the core of a dream. And you think money lies at the core of your wants. And that's what you have in common with every other person that reads this book. That is your collective consciousness. You think money is the answer to all of your prayers. Some of you would even buy love for a day or two with money.

The dream of not having money, in your consciousness, is a limitation.

It is limited **thought**. As long as that thought sits inside of you, you will never become a Christ. And becoming a Christ is the epic destiny of man.

*"It's like the world and all its
possibilities lay there waiting for us to. . ."*
"Yes?"
" 'Create' them. Touch them alive."
*"What makes us create certain realities
and leave others?" asked Valerie.
I considered my answer before speaking.
"I'm not sure. But I think it has something
to do with what a person **believes** to be
true. . . to be real."
"I think a person sees, or 'creates'
what he believes. I mean **really** believes,
not just **wishes** to be true. A lot of people
wish they were rich. But the people who
really believe they deserve to be rich,
are rich."*

Trick of the Light

Requiem for a Dreamer

Don't you realize that you create the destiny in front of you? Don't you know that what you lust for, and envy, and want, and need, and dream about, and think about is unfulfilled destiny? And don't you know that it is only when you fulfill those destinies that you are free of them?

A manifestation in front of you is not a miracle of manifestation. It is a miracle of relief!

For only when the dream has been realized does it no longer eat at you. Only when it has been realized does it no longer own you. The moment it is manifested into the material world is the moment it gives you up. It's up for sale.

I have been teaching you "all of these years," that the path to the Kingdom of Heaven is the Within Path. It is called the path of Joy.

You can run around laughing like a ninny poopkincake, saying "Indeed, indeed, indeed, I am God, I am God," but it won't get you around your dreams that still live in your heart, even though you try to ignore them.

You can't ignore unfulfilled dreams. Trying to ignore unfulfilled dreams with intellectual but unowned spiritual dogma is called pious hypocrisy. No one ever got what I told them. No one realized what the runner meant. Joy! What does the path look like? Maybe I used too many "Indeed, so be its."

I'm clarifying it now.

The path is called **self joy**. But you haven't really looked at that. Instead you have hopped on someone else's path. You are, by and large, all path-jumpers, guru-hoppers, teacher-followers.

And you will never learn, not until you look
within *and* **know***.*

The path to the Kingdom of Heaven is within and it is called
joy. Read carefully now, this is important. We are talking about
how your destiny is created here.

When you embrace your outermost dreams of
limitation into fruition within your soul, they
will manifest in front of you. What is embraced
emotionally, in the soul, will manifest in front
of you.

It is called destiny. And on this plane, destiny is controlled by
time, distance, space, and velocity of life. You are in a time flow.

Your mind is in the future. Your emotions are in the now. And
your body is in the past. That's how you live.

Now, let's look at the surface layers of your life and how you
deal with them. What are they? Here's an example. You say, "I
want to cut my hair off, but I cannot because my lover adores it,
and I hate it. But if I cut it off, the crowning glory of God, not only
will I be a sinner, but my husband/lover may find another." And
so you wash and comb and brush with a flurry.

What sort of dream is that?

The dream behind that original statement is, "I would like to be
free of this hair." But what holds you back is, "I'm afraid I won't
be loved any longer if I do what I want, instead of what someone
else wants me to do." So the original dream stays in the soul,
unrealized. Are you getting this?

What about the artist who has the ability to work under a grand
creative genius? He just knows that if he had the chance, the
genius could create a lot more. But he is afraid to show his genius
because it would threaten his position. I do believe you call it
politics. So, instead, he lives with a latent talent that is not used.
You see? After all, you aren't supposed to make waves. Mustn't
muddy the water.

Then there is the woman who lives with her husband, but in her heart she feels no passion. She desires secretly to be free to come and go when she pleases, to eat whenever, to lie with him when she wishes to lie, rather than upon command. But she doesn't fulfill her desire because her husband is her provider. What would her children say if she left? What would happen to her? Leaving, she thinks, couldn't be worth the guilt she would feel. So, she becomes a suppressed old woman.

Dreams unfulfilled.

You will never become The Lord God of Your Being while you are hung up on unhappiness.

I see many of you dream of having an idea of your own, of being a fulfilled creative person, of being inventive, of having an invention of yours **out there**, appreciated in the world. But the dream is inhibited by the lack of gold. So you return to your nine to five and you live feeling a foiled genius, while your dream hangs there over you.

Then there are those of you that genuinely desire to be unhappy. You really want to be miserable, wretched, and despicable, like your fantasies are, vile and bigoted. You'd really like to be all of those things, but you don't dare to be those things because, "Good heavens, what would people think? Straight Joe Blow, unhappy?" So, you hide your innermost feelings, too. And you put on the smile. And you clean your fingernails and shave the hair from your face. And you become a hypocrite. You want to be unhappy, but no one said it was all right. In your culture it is a "no-no." "Be happy!"

There are many emotions that are unspeakable in your culture. Why do you think your psychiatrists are so well off? Because the unspeakables have to go to someone who will speak to them! And after years and years of rehashing it, you are still not happy. You know why? Because your psychiatrist never said, "It's all right. Go out and be despicable."

And then there are those of you who want to be happy, but you hold onto all of the reasons you're not. You want to be skinny, but you eat yourself into oblivion every time you think about it. You want to be beautiful, but every time you look in the mirror, you hate what you see. You want to laugh and be joyous, but that's vulgar.

> *That's the duality. You want it, but you think you don't deserve it.*

You live in a duality. So unfulfilled dreams and desires hang in the soul as confusion. And what inevitably happens to you is that you wind up like most of you are right now. You end up running amuck trying to find someone in your life to give you balance and purpose. You need, you want, to have someone to share this misery with, so that they can take the brunt of the confusion and the hurt. You want someone to tolerate the psychotic attitude and to still sit there and smile at you and lovingly say, "You're wonderful. Wonderful. Wonderful!"

It's called putting the blame on someone else.

There are many more "for instances" I could use, examples of your unfulfilled dreams that hang over you.

I hope you know by now that I am not talking about your nocturnal dreams where knights in shining armour gallop across clear waters and through daisy and poppy-covered fields of forever to find the woman whose hair drags the ground and who wears a loose girdle. I am not speaking of those dreams!

I am speaking of the dreams of suppressed fulfillment, whatever they may be.

Joy is not defined in terms of your laws. Joy reaches beyond the laws. Joy is what you have lost. You have what your civilization would call "prudent lifestyles," but you have more crime and viciousness and murder and rape and war and hideous behavior than ever before.

And then there is the soldier who uses his tongue to carve away the innocence of another. And yet, your society is called modern, Christian, God-fearing. You should fear some of those Gods!

*Joy is the relief from suppression. It is what
allows you to go **beyond**, to be what you want
to be. It only takes a moment to reach that
place where the dream gives you up.*

And there is a joy that comes in that moment of release. I once said, "I will open your doors and clean out your closets, your souls, with one shiny burnished thing. Joy."

The lack of joy is the reason you are grumbling in the murk and mire and living despicable lives, because the dreams that you have stuffed away in your closets were to be the catalyst to experience, resulting in joy.

"You're living with your brain and not your senses. Your senses, unclouded and unabused, are the compass of the soul. You live in the past, seeing what you want to see. You see the world through dead eyes."

Trick of the Light

Being a Christ Is Living What You Are

What is reality?

What lies in front of you and tantalizes your senses? You know—touching, feeling, smelling.

Emotion is the true power, the coagulation of a manifestation that adorns the senses. That is the reality. Without emotion there are no senses; without emotion, there is nothing.

You want to have money. You want to have it all. But you can never have it all, nor can you pass this plane a happy man, until you have at least realized what blocks you.

Do you know what it means to be **blocked**? Blockage occurs when what you desire doesn't happen. And you say, "I am blocked." Why are you blocked? Because there is a dream sitting there, a dream of a possible adventure that you have not embraced.

Why do you suppose I call Yeshua Ben Joseph a noble Christ? What is there to that word noble? Virtuous and noble. Of noble virtue. What does that mean? The quality of a Christ does not mean a suppression of what you are. It means living what you are, until it gives you up. The more dreams you realize, the more "vacant" you become inside; only then is there room to see the light.

A being of noble virtue is one who has lived all of his limitations, meaning all of his dreams. And when they are all gone, that is the moment he becomes the Christ. And when he walks he leaves no track, for there is nothing to leave. Everything has given him up. Do you understand? If you don't understand this, you are going to run around to a lot of teachers with your hands held out, just hoping that you wore your good-luck charm or whatever it takes to be blessed that day, and you are going to be sorely disappointed.

You people seem to be tantalized by those individuals who seem to own it all. Why, you even prostrate yourselves before them! Don't you know you own it all? It isn't that just some special entities came here, lived here, and then were resurrected. It was that they understood that the way back home and the way to the greatest kingdom of all was through God within. That is the path to opening the power to become all things.

Why do you think Yeshua Ben Joseph, the Christ, went into the desert to be tempted by Satan for forty days? Who was Satan? The Satan that tempted the Christ was his alter ego. And what was this temptation? To be powerful enough to rule the world. In those days in the desert, Yeshua saw before Him the cities of Persia, Rome, and Ethiopia. He saw Mesopotamia, the old Hittites. And he saw the formidable Egyptians. Every kingdom appeared before him because that was what lay there for him to experience.

Satan within is the alter ego in its need.

Christ saw them all and embraced every one of them. He saw them. He tasted them. He was them. And they gave him up in forty days. What was the dream? Temptation. What is temptation? Temptation is a suppressed dream. It is when you realize your dreams, when you have faced them and owned them, that they are no longer temptation. And only then are those blocks no longer there inside you.

What is it to forgive what you call a sinner? It is to understand that there are limitations, dreams, that must be owned to be free of them. Do you understand? Why was this necessary for Yeshua Ben Joseph? Because without it, Masters, he could not be what he desired to be above all things. And His Kingdom was not of this world.

Now, what is the difference between you and Him?

Only motivation. You would rather fuss, cuss, argue, feel limited, and run around chasing your tail being altogether unhappy than to spend one moment in recognition of who you are. That is because you lack the motivation to find joy.

Now, what does this have to do with finances? Everything. Everyone reading this book has an obsessive dream for gold. If I gave you a gift that was shimmering, bright, and beauteous, it would be falling into a hand that is malicious, unhappy, and miserable, and the energy of that hand alone changes the power.

Doors can open with opportunity, but if you're not motivated, what is going to get you up off your rear and make you go through the door? You'd rather sit there and whine and cry because nothing happened.

Now, I've done wondrous things. But I already know I leave no tracks. I will give you the power of knowledge and a strong wind at your back for motivation. But only you can turn that toward **self** and face your dreams. I cannot make you. There are many people in this world who are ignorant about your government and the world at large. They are followers and whiners. There are people that, through their own ignorance, depend completely on someone else to make every decision in their life. They have no drive. They are rather more like a blob. They wait for someone to prod them and move them on to the next place in life.

Now, what do I mean by that? Only that a lot of people want everyone to do everything for them. So, **they** never know. They will have to come back in another lifetime to deal with the dreams which are their limitations.

Each of you reading this has dreams that hang in your soul. Why couldn't you see the light? Why didn't you have the vision? Why couldn't you heal yourself? What about all of those mythological miracles that you hear about great masters performing in far-off places? They exist. Why can't you do them? Because you want to make one major leap from starting way **out there**, all the way **inside** to the light. And you know what else I've observed about your behavior? If you don't see the light, you'll swear that you did just to look good in front of your friends.

You want to bypass every dream to get there. Do you know what has happened, illusionary entities, whose fantasies truly are ecstasies? I've now created another dream for you—going home, enlightenment. And now you have placed this dream in front of all those old dreams and you're further stuck than ever before! You have to get beyond all that to get back down to the "nitis gritis" of facing your original dreams.

So we'd better get down to work.

The first runner you will encounter after working with this material is for those of you who are not aware of your limitations.

Now, look here, when I say limitations, I don't mean the kind of limitation where you have your hands tied, and therefore your ability to move is restricted. I am speaking of the limitation created because you have overbooked your soul with desires, dreams, and hang-ups, to such an extent that you don't know where to begin to unravel it all. You will soon encounter a person who will allow you to clearly view your first unfulfilled dream; so you know what your first limitation is.

There are three parts to this experience of encounter.

This experience is for those who've lost sight of their first limitation, their first unfulfilled dream. (So, you will encounter three runners that are all part of one experience.)

This first person will represent your unfulfilled dream. This individual will be very pompous. They'll brag about where they are in life. They'll brag about achieving the dream, about their wealth, about how much food they have, about how much land they're going to buy. They will brag about everything that sticks in your craw. You won't be able to miss this person; it will be very obvious.

The second aspect of this experience is an invitation from this person to hook up. When I say hook up, I mean they will say, "Come along and dance on my lightship." In other words, a door will open to allow you the opportunity of experiencing your dream.

To make this next aspect to this sequence happen, you must have gone with the individual you encountered and the door that opens. Next you will meet a person who will facilitate the open door, sort of a doorman to open the door. This can only occur if you recognize the mirror held before you and see the door.

There is a hitch. You must embrace and accept. By the way, do you know what embracing is? Some of you call it envy.

You know those emotions. Jealousy and envy. "Why, that so and so, who does he think he is? Does he think he's God or something?" And what you're really saying is, "I AM, and he's got everything I want."

You must go on a little adventure to fulfill this dream. I am simply helping you along in realization.

Now, where is all this getting those of you who are saying, "Give it to me. Just give it to me and shut up." I know how you think, and I have a special little experience for you. You are going to get just what you want. And only when you realize getting what you think you want hasn't made you happy, will you begin the other experience of dream realization.

Financial freedom comes from unlocking the genius in what you are.

Every entity that has gained his gold has gained it through a rarity called common sense. That is what I call genius. And it is genius that also leads back to God.

What are you looking for? I can help you find what you're looking for, but I can't make you hold onto it. Tell me how much gold you want and I will tell you that figure will never be enough. You will always want more.

Teaching you how to manifest is part of what we're going to do here. But you can't begin to manifest until you recognize why you can't make it happen right now. These first runners are to get you going. After that, it's sort of a "difficult breeze," because what it means is that you must take responsibility for the light that is hidden within. Realizing all of your dreams is imperative to getting what you want.

" 'I gave you twenty non-negotiable pieces
of paper and suddenly you were happy.'
'So?'
'What made you happy?'
'The twenty grand.'
'But the twenty grand never really existed.'
'But I was led to believe it did.'
'Still, even though it didn't really exist,
you were still happy.'
'Because I thought it was real.'
'What **really** made you happy, Nick?' said
Sam, interrupting me.
Then it just slipped out. 'I did.' The
counterfeit money had maintained its real
value throughout. It was just that when I held
it in my hands I created all kinds of scenarios
in my mind that gave me a sense of pleasure and
well-being. I know this might be hard to swallow,
but I suddenly got a whole different perspective
on money."

Trick of the Light

If Every One of Your Dreams Is Based on Money, You Are in for a Rude Awakening

I will teach you how to manifest from the Lord God of Your Being—not the gold, but the dreams. And if you take the knowledge you have gained thus far and live this truth to the letter, allowing your narrow mind to open up just a wee bit, you will understand. It will become very clear and you will **realize** every dream that you had when you began this book.

Every dream realized gives you up and you can go home to a kingdom that is beyond words.

In other words, it is not gold that makes it happen, but pure love.

Do you know what the word "attitude" means? Let's see, you could have a bad attitude, a good attitude, a positive attitude, a bummer attitude. The understanding that you are God gets buried underneath the dreams. But what gave the dreams credence in the first place? What gave gold credence? The Father within you. So you created every single one of those little things that are hanging there. But with what sort of attitude did you create them? What sort of knowingness?

There is something you need to know about the men who use religion to gain control. What they really want is power. And when I tell you of men who amass gold, what they really want is power. What they all want is to have the power to ultimately control human destiny. And those powerful people despise you, because to them, you are the rabble in the marketplace. You only exist to be manipulated and worked through.

Why does that attitude exist? Because it desires to exist. After all, they are only gods just like you, and it is their dream to be powerful and controlling. Do you understand? It is necessary to learn this.

I know there are a lot of you reading this thinking, "That isn't me. I'm not into control. I just want a better-paying job." You don't fool anybody. You're just trying to clean up the picture. The attitude is what tells the truth.

Let's look at your attitude about gold and dollars. (And by the way, if I had to pick between gold and dollars, I would recommend gold.)

How do I teach you that it is far greater to replace that desire for gold with a desire for genius? Don't you know the mind creates everything? And you're thinking, "Good teaching, Ramtha, but I don't think it's in my dream." I am telling you this for a reason.

If every one of your dreams is based on money and the stock market, you are in for a rude awakening. Are you with me? Don't run out the door and sell your stocks. Listen to what I am saying. I am saying that if your future and all of your dreams depend on the stock market and on your investments, you are on tenuous footing.

And if you are grumbling about what you may have to invest for your food, one day you will sit down and kiss the ground you are sitting on, because money, as a commodity by itself, backed in dreams, is fallible to the men who control it.

It's not your money. It is owned by the Federal Reserve. And did you think that was owned by your government? The Federal Reserve is owned by the most powerful families since the hour of Napoleon. And they are not about to give it up.

My desire is to educate you; so here it is. Your paper money is owned by the men who created it. Your government is owned. Every government, with the exception of India, is owned by world bankers. Didn't you know that? Are you shocked? Once you are aware of that, you can begin to assess what it is you really want.

You need to select a dream that is not so fallible. You need to have a dream which can be brought to fruition; one that is backed up, so it can be realized, so it can give you up and you can go on to the next realization. A dream realized is one that can back itself up. In being realized, it gives you up, so you can go on to the next realization. That is the pattern of life and the road home.

When the rich man comes down from the tower, it doesn't own him any longer. When the poor man gives up his rags and goes to the tower, the rags don't own him any longer. He is ready for the next level of understanding. If you say you are a spiritual entity, you have to have the gall to say that all things are spirit.

If you say you are a spiritual entity, then you must have the brain mass to realize that everyone else out there is God too! And that everyone is creating their destiny. They have made it the way they wanted to make it. Governments and international powers sit on your wondrous emerald globe as players on a chess game. And the one who pulls the strings owns the money. Your government doesn't go to war because of noble virtue. It goes to war because it's good business.

Open up here. Let your brain become activated, and ask to receive a greater thought that will help you understand your limitations—which are the same as your dreams, of course. It is nonsense to say, "I AM the Lord God of My Being and I don't want to know anything else." It is absurd to say, "My lower and higher self are not in agreement." That is a deterrent to reality. Arguing with yourself doesn't make you aware of your dreams. It doesn't bring you closer to your unlimited self, which is where you need to be.

Think long and hard about this information. This is pure reason. Pure knowingness. And it is very simple to obtain this understanding if you allow yourself to get beyond your limited mind and embrace it.

Instead of the core of your dream being money, it is far smarter to desire to manifest what the money would buy, rather than going through the money to buy it, except for those of you who would like to wear your desire around your neck. Then your desire is fulfilled threefold. It is usable gold in the days to come, it is a manifested dream, and it shines!

This monkey-mind you live with—your alter ego/social consciousness—has programmed in this business of obtaining wealth. Wealth, to you, means the accumulation of assets and money. But assets are only good if they can be liquidated into the bottom line.

Now, when gold ceased to back up the paper, the consciousness of your alter ego became affected. It is pure reasoning. Go back to the greatest teaching of all, that you are God.

You are God!

That means that all of the I AM is GOD. Forever and ever and ever. And once you embrace that, and **know** it, if you simply desire what you want, without money, you will get it. Lickety-split!

Why am I telling you to desire the thing you want, not the money to buy it? Because you are poverty-conscious people. You never have enough money.

What do you and your lover fight about? What do you gripe about to your children? They spend too much. Everything centers around money. What is your saying? Money is the root of all evil?

Reason it out for yourself. (That's when you learn best.) If you think this is the only life you have ever lived, born of this world, destined by God to live and die, with even the hour of your death known, then there is evil. And it exists because if that short span, not even a **breath** in the face of all eternity, is all you call life, then certainly there is evil.

Knowing you are forever transcends evil because there is no such thing. There is only God. The experience of life is continuum. If the experience of your life is only short-lived, in a struggle of moving from here to there, then it is governed by evil, and there is a constant struggle to pull away from that evil and to try to be perpetually good. Those who control you have created this concept for the power that gives them over you. Don't you see? As long as they have you believing in evil, they have the power to say **when** in your life.

Allow your knowingness to know. The more you know, in innocence, the greater you will be able to use your knowingness. For your knowingness is the Father Within, the Lord God of Your Being, and you can call it forth from any direction. The wind comes from many directions, not just one. The answer to your dreams does not hang onto the premise called gold. But you have to change your **attitude,** because to you, your world evolves around gold.

And as long as you see it that way,
so it will be for you.

And the "realist" sits there with his arms folded and says, "But this is the real world here. I have to pay my electric bill!" But the God says, "I AM THE ALL THAT IS THE WORLD."

When you change your attitude about hungering for gold, and embrace the dream that sits inside you, and let **that** be what you give credence to, you will see your dreams manifested rapidly before your eyes, because it has come from a place that has no blocks, no hang-ups, no difficulties.

You see something beautiful in the store and you ask how much it costs. Everything centers around price. As long as it does, those illusions will hide the dreams. Your attitude tells you, "I can't have it because it's too much money."

Change the attitude! Go unlimited! Embrace! To embrace what it is you want, you must make it naked. It costs nothing to embrace the dream within, and in that moment of high emotion you are allowed to live your dream of what you want.

How do I make myself clearer?

Here's one you might understand. Men, what do you do if you want an erection? You fantasize about the moment that gives you lust and passion. In your mind, you live that moment and your body responds. That is called manifestation. Your body manifests a response to the pictures and feeling in your mind. That process works that quickly because you **know** you can make that happen! Now, if we place a woman with nipples the color of rosehips right in front of you, you might not be so sure about yourself! But all alone in the dark, you can create! (I cannot help but laugh at you sometimes!)

Your body is beautiful. It is a wonder, and for a vivid example that brings this concept home clearly to you, there is no better. That is how powerful you are.

In a moment you can create an emotion and create a reaction to that emotion. And in the spilling forth of the seed, the burden is given up. It no longer owns you. Do you understand the example? It is nature. It is marvelous. Wondrous!

In God, there is no split energy. Even negative and positive are one. And the same is true of their opposites. Energy is energy. God didn't create greater emphasis on the atom than He did the sun. It is the same. The illusion is it's separation. It is the same. In a moment, through emotion, you could embrace the dream without the gold. In a moment, you could live it vividly in emotional expression, and by the law that all things come into fruition from the emotional being, so does it manifest. Why? Because there is nothing that blocks it. It doesn't cost anything. It just IS. Pure energy.

Now in the current reigning attitude, or what I call **social consciousness**, the ultimate controller of power is money. That is limited consciousness being expressed on a grand scale. If you transcend that limited consciousness that says you need the money, and go simply to the object, it becomes yours. You see? Because everyone owns already what you want in gold. Did you know that?

What I am saying is, the money isn't yours.

You understand? It isn't yours. You do not have the dominion over it. It belongs to someone else and you are in debt to them. That is how your society works.

If you embrace the dream, simply for what the dream is itself, and live it to a peak of emotion, as you do your sexuality, that dream by law will manifest.

For the glory of God, it will **become**. And the more you own these dreams, the quicker you feel that joy and you get closer to coming home.

Home is not walking forward; **it is going within**. And every dream releases you more so you can do just that.

Rich man, when your nights are lonely, why aren't you happy? What lies behind the surface? What is it you want now? Oh! Greedy entity. Don't you see? You desired the money, not the emotion you hoped the money would buy. If you wanted love, you should have desired **love**, not **money**.

"What happened to her?"
"Funny you should ask," replied Susie. "Said
she'd found God."
*"I've got this week's **TV Guide** at home. Did*
she happen to mention what channel He was on?"

Trick of the Light

You Do Not Live in the State of California! You Live in a State Called Poverty Consciousness!

You are poverty-conscious people, and you don't know how to get out of it. Give to Caesar what is Caesar's, but own what is eternal; that is your inherited right. And if you are still waiting for someone to flop it in your hands, you'll run out very shortly.

It only takes one manifestation of a dream to make you fully realize and completely own what I said in the beginning.

Big deal! The Kingdom of Heaven is within! Big deal, that you are God! It must be **lived**. It only takes one manifestation that you embrace, that you create, to set you going home. It only takes that taste of primeval power to make you realize you can do it. And then the game is no longer how much gold you amass in your dream, or how many objects. (And remember about objects: they can only be worth something if they can be sold.)

The secret is that you need to taste the power of what it is to be a Master coming Home. And then you will no longer be saying, "I need the land. I need the food. I need the gold." You will begin to manifest all of your dreams, and the more you do, the more powerful you become. Then it is a release. Then you will be capable of saying, "I am hungry," and in the moment you create the stillness, the manna comes.

You don't have to say, "I want the dollar to buy the bread." In future times, they won't give you the dollar. So make the bread. Get it?

Then you'll walk like a Master.

And every dream **peeled,** layer by layer, every dream that gives you up, will take you closer to what every great Master since the beginning of your time has said. **The power is within you! You can do anything, for God that you are is forever and, indeed, eternal!**

But the trick is to get you to rebirth, through knowledge, this attitude you have about money. I cannot make you do it. I can send the runners of understanding—those fleet-footed beings that help you learn through trial, mayhem, joy, whatever it takes!

I can do many things to make you think about it. I've watched people lose all of their gold, and they cursed me and hated me. That's how much this understanding has cost some. Some have had to come to a point of nakedness, so that they have to create. You have to get off of your divine rear ends and want it bad enough to do it. And then you crawl back up.

Necessity is the mother of invention. It is also termed the greater genius. How could you be a genius if everything had been thought of? Well, it hasn't, not by a long shot. It's just that much of the current genius has been controlled by government and industry. But it will not always be that way.

Now, what am I encouraging you to manifest? If we remove money, what lies at the core of your dream?

It is called genius.

Genius is begotten of the Father. When you decide to remove this narrow-mindedness about you, to remove social consciousness, when that gets out of the way, an unlimited mind is born. And it is that unlimited mind that is the heart of God. And that mind, through genius, creates all manifestations.

And it doesn't cost you anything.

How do you do it? You have already started to do it because you have desired to know and started the process of learning. And some of you will get your money, because that's all you can imagine wanting. But it will run out. And, then again, maybe you will listen to the meaning intoned in what I say, and you will try to manifest something other than money.

I have never been a compromiser. Do you know what a compromiser is? It is a spiritual prostitute. They would have you view them as angels of light, when they are really hypocrites in their soul. They compromise. You compromise.

It is the truth that will set you free, coupled with an understanding of social consciousness, which is the fickleness of man and his nature.

I know how your mind works. I can hear you now. You would say to me, "Beloved brother, 'tis I, working from the Lord God of my Being."

And I would say to you, "At what cost, Master?"

And you would say back, "The cost doesn't matter. I desire this. I want." And then you turn around and ask, "And, by the way, what should I invest in?"

What was the first understanding in the above passage? I desire to be God. And for a moment, that which fulfills was seen, but lost in the next moment.

You must reach the place where "I want to become God" is the grandest desire of all. For it is only when one hungers, do you learn through the mother of invention. Only when you are going broke do you begin to grope and become inventive, frantic, panicked, hissing, hating, malicious. Only then do you get down to the very core of your being to replace your treasure.

And, by George, you do it! And then you say, "No thanks to you."

And I say, "Of course!"

Compromise. How can you say, "I want to be God," and then want to know what to invest in? Is that not a cancellation of thoughts and wishes?

What you are saying is, "I want to be rich, so I have the time to be God."

Spare me.

I owe no man on this plane anything. I have no regrets of anything I have ever taught, individually or collectively. My truth is an even truth. It is not tainted. It is not glossed over. It just is, like a pregnant dream lying there. Why? Because I own it all already. Why would I hold a dream of compromise? I own it. My life owned it.

I am a staunch teacher.

But if you can take it in, through your alter ego, and listen to what I am saying with the light of your own pure reason, there will come an hour when you will be owned by no man. And you can be the light of the morning. And you will be integrity and honor; and the beauty that you are will leave no shadow.

Compromising entities leave thick shadows.

It comes back to your legacy.

The legacy is that you are God! And the Father and you are One. And the Kingdom of Heaven is within you. And if you say, "I desire to become God," then what is it to break down all of social consciousness until you understand each fragment and own it? So what if it means you grapple with every aspect of your character? So what if it means you celebrate every aspect of your character?

It makes no difference what is necessary to come to that hour that you change your attitude! That is what it takes. Bless whatever it takes to get you there!

There are very wealthy entities that despise me because they lost part of their fortunes because of me. But I love them. They have grown balls. That is your term, isn't it? You use it colloquially to imply true grit, to resurrect.

You learn out of your own genius. That is wondrous. That is how it must be! There will come an hour when the dream of hate and maliciousness and bitterness and anger is owned, and it will give you up.

And how will that happen? When that rich person becomes to someone else just what I became to him. Then, when they are hated and despised and rebuked, all of a sudden they will own it. They will become impeccable, and they will compromise no more.

It is a series of grand teachings and lessons to help you to understand the game that you call reality. This is all to help you. It is all to get you on the other side of it. Get it? I love you!

My desire is for you to have sovereignty.

For in the days that lie hanging in the future, sovereignty and impeccability are truth. And if you live your truth, nothing will smite you or hurt you; and you will not hunger, for that is the reality of a virtuous, uncompromising entity.

"You're not suggesting that just by changing the way we think about things, the world changes," I said skeptically. "Positive thinking is nothing new." "I'm recommending thinking less and perceiving more."

Trick of the Light

The Old Man And The Magi

Once there was an man, sort of like you without the cosmetics and jewels and fine linens and silks and all of that. He was just a plain old entity who wanted to own it all.

(This is a true story, by the way.)

This man went to a Magi and said, "Magi, I want to have a kingdom. What should I do?"

The Magi sent him to the tallest mountain in the whole country with these instructions, "Go to this mountain and gather rocks and build a hovel on the mountain, and you shall have a kingdom to see all of the world from."

This Magi was the wisest in the land, so the man took the advice. This man was also particularly generous. He gave a ruble to the beggar who begs for alms, bought himself a sweetmeat, packed up his ass, and headed for the mountain.

He went high up the mountain, and the gods must have been with him, for nigh, it didn't snow for a whole season. And he gathered up all of the ancient rocks, and with the dung from his wondrous animal, he stuck the rocks together and made himself a hovel. And as the grasses began to dry from the reeds, he went and picked them. And he thatched them and put a roof on. And since there wasn't a lot of wood about, he took the dung, dried it, and it made fuel.

And he had a view! Ah! What a view.

He sat there for a while enjoying the view and eating his meager crumbs. But when he realized that nothing was really happening, he got back on his ass and went back down to the Magi. He said "Magi, I want my kingdom. I've already done what you instructed."

And the Magi looked at him and said to him, "Now, go and tear it all down and put the rocks back where you found them."

Well, the man was incredulous. Really. But then a thought came to him, like all of you think. "If I do this, maybe I'll get the castle of gold." So he convinced himself that his labor of putting all of the rocks back just meant that he was going to have a shiny gold palace.

You see, that was his motivation.

So he packed his ass, gave the beggar a ruble, went back up the mountain, and began to take apart everything he had built. The reeds came off of the roof, and one by one, he took all of the rocks off. And all the while he worked, he busied himself by trying to remember the exact location of each particular rock. He had a fervor to do it perfectly, because he just knew that if he did it precisely correct, he would have his palace of shining gold. So you know, he didn't mind stretching his memory a bit on where everything went. Small sacrifice.

And when he was all done, he had a pleasant but coarse evening meal. Then he got on his ass and went back to see the Magi. As he passed on the way to the Magi, there was that same beggar crying for alms, alms, alms.

Well, he gave him one coin and then found the Magi, who said, "Go and find every rock you put back and rebuild the hovel, just as you had built it before."

Third time is a charm.

The Magi only smiled. The man sighed very deeply. Well, you can imagine. He walked outside and ignored the beggar screaming for alms. Funds were getting low. So, he packed up his ass, went back up to the mountain, found every rock just the way he had left them, and began to work rebuilding.

Well, about three quarters of the way up with this rock and dung wall, he realized what he was doing here. And he decided that if he showed perseverance, he would be rewarded by Allah. So he increased his pace, all the while singing a little tune. The whole valley echoed. The ass looked up, paid him little attention, and went back to eating and making more dung on all the rocks.

So the man continued getting everything precise. But before he was a quarter of the way done, a horrid snowstorm blew in.

Well, a little snowstorm was not going to deter the coming of Shamballah!

So, he covered himself up a little bit closer, put the ass in the center of the house, and continued putting up his reeds in a blazing snow storm.

When he was all done, he was shivering. He made a meager fire. The ass simply stared at him with glossy brown, dewy eyes, and he, of himself, was content.

The man was getting a little angry. He had done a lot for Allah. Every day he talked to Allah. Every day he pleaded with Allah. Surely Allah knew what a servant he had there? Didn't he know that out of the charity of his being, he had done everything precisely as the Magi had said, and could not Allah smile on him and give him, oh, say, some property in Malibu? (I had to update the story, you know.)

The snowstorm was all settled. Allah was mute as ever.

The man packed up his ass and went back down to see the Magi.

The Magi said, "Ahhhhhhh, Ahhhhh. You have done very well. Just a little bit longer. Go and tear it all down and put all of the rocks back precisely where you found them."

"You gotta be kidding? Magi, what have you been smoking?" (Another contemporizing. You do say that, I've heard you!) And the Magi assured him this was just for a little bit longer.

Well, he got up and dragged his ass to the ass. And when the beggar called for, "Alms! Alms!" he spit in his eye, because he realized the beggar had gotten very wealthy and he was only poorer.

And he went on his merry way in not so merry a mood. On this particular day, he did not whistle a tune.

No longer did he look up with faintly hypocritical eyes spewing forth salty tears in the name of love for Allah. He just looked at the sun that had hurt his eyes. Saffron dust was now settling thickly over his being. He coughed and choked himself up to the mountain.

You know, you can only hand Allah so much when you are

feeling good. When you don't feel so hot, it ain't Allah anymore. It's just the dreadful noonday sun beating down on you and your poor ass.

So he went back up the mountain, but right away, he noticed he was not immediately motivated, shall we say, to get back to putting all these rocks back where they came from. You see, by now he knew where every rock went on the mountainside and he could move them blindfolded.

And so he sat there on the ground with his mind going, "I know where you go and where you go."

"You go there. You go here."

"You go over there. You come back to here. You go down there. And you go back up this way."

"It's slippery, but you go there."

And he sat there and in his mind every rock went back in place. He was really exasperated, very weary just from going through the procedure. He hadn't lifted a finger.

So he hopped on his ass and went down to the Magi.

And the Magi says, "Have you removed every stone?"

And he says, "Indeed."

"Then you must go back one more time and build it."

"I already have."

And the Magi says, "Well, then, tear it down."

He said, "I just did."

So what happened to the house? Well, there came a dreadful snowstorm that blew the roof off, and eventually, because it was so cold, the dung froze up, became brittle, and all the stones rolled off the house. And they sat there under a thick blanket of snow for the rest of the winter.

Well, of course, when the spring thaw came, there was an avalanche that went down the mountain. As the avalanche went down the mountain, all of those stones that he had so deliciously, meticulously placed came rolling down the mountain and split open. A few of them hit him in his ass!

In the center of one of the stones was the mother lode.

Inside every rock that came down from the mountain was what

was called yellow fever. Gold. Every one of those rocks he had put up had a gold vein in it. I am not going to tell you exactly where the place is, but I'll give you a clue.

Solomon got his share.

Now, the moral of the story—to help you along here—is that the dreams are just like the building of this hovel. There will come an hour when it is no longer what you manifest outside of you, but what you have done inside of you, and the moment that the outside no longer exists for the plane of demonstration, it is the inside that relieves us of all of our burdens. The dreams. And it's going to take an awful lot of runners and experiences. And it will demand every one of your dreams going back and forth, doing them over and over and over until you can say, "I already have."

Only when it is that quickened will you be able to see the Lord God of your Being sitting there like a brilliant flame. And what now becomes in **here**, inside, is owned in a moment and the after-effect is like an avalanche.

It was there all along in those stones.

You have to do this in order to be able to say, "I already have." You have to be able to have this dream and to demonstrate the things you need in order to say, "I already have." And that is the purpose of this book. Financial Freedom.

And by the time you have finished this book, that will simply mean **freedom**.

So be it.

One of these days I'll tell that story and you'll really understand, because you will have owned it.

*"I started to look around and see life as
a dream. As a choice that I made, created, and
literally brought into existence. And while
all other possibilities or choices are avail-
able, they're simply not 'chosen.' They lie
dormant . . . 'unchosen.' They are 'unrealized'
realities."*

Trick of the Light

Beginning the Process By Remembering the Dream

W hat do you need? What do you want?

It is time to begin the process of looking within to find your dreams. After this chapter, I want you to go and take a moment to address your bodily needs. Relieve yourself and then fill yourself back up, so that as you start to look within, your body isn't distracting you.

Then I want you to find a quiet, alone place. Take your pen and paper to this alone place, and once you are settled, I want you to ask from the Lord God of Your Being what it is that you want. Go as deep inside as you can and capture in liquid script all the things that you desire.

In other words, write down all your dreams.

Why am I asking you to do that? Because I know when you do this now, in the light of the new knowledge you have gained thus far, you will see your dreams from a different perspective. You have to. You are sensitive people. And you have to write them down to know they exist. This time, see the dream changing the core. Just write from the **"I want"** perspective.

You can list as many as you want. Or you can list only one. You can still simply write down, "It's just money. That's all I want." That's all right. But this is how you get to that place where one day you have gained enough to be magnificent and you can say, "I already have. I own it."

We are about to undertake the process through which you make your dreams happen.

All you need is one eensy, teensy, weensy manifestation. You just need to make one thing that you dreamed of come true to give you a taste of **the Father and I are One.**

If you need a rest to get better in touch with your dreams, so to speak, take your rest. But before you continue this book, if you wish to work with the process, be in knowledge of your dreams, the limitations of your being.

*"But doesn't this kind of thinking
create a type of psychological anarchy
where nothing is bad and it's every person
for himself?"*
*"That type of 'thinking' might—that type of
seeing would not."*

Trick of the Light

Survival or Arrival—
You Choose

If you have contemplated your dreams in the light of this new information, then you now can see them as limitations that are holding you back. And perhaps you have surmised without my needing to tell you, that if you are laden with dreams, then you are not ready to go home.

After all, what is life?

It is the grand platform through which God the Father keeps life perpetuating forward, evolving, becoming grander, changing. God isn't perfect in this plane and perfection is a dream.

Let me ask you something? Why do you have this life if you desire to leave it straightaway? Through your drama, you can dream the dreams and then bring them into reality. That's what this is all for! It is not for you to come to this earth and be obstinate and abstinent. That is boring! You are missing the whole boat and the picture entirely.

It is also a limitation to view the love of God as a restriction to life. It does not make any sense at all that there should be **God** and then there should be **life** and that you should ignore life in order to serve God. That would be a hypocrisy. God and life are not separate. What other purpose would you be here for, but to experience all of life? **Think about it.**

You are forever entities. You are! And your dreams are but phases of evolution.

And until you realize the dreams, you do not evolve.

Great is the Master who comes into his Christhood because he has evolved through his dreams of need. If the soul feels the need, it means you should own it, regardless of what it is.

It is when dreams are suppressed that anger, violence, and wicked deeds are perpetrated. Don't you understand that? Wicked deeds happen when you suppress dreams!

If you really allowed yourself to fully embrace the understanding of what I have said thus far, you could find joy. But that is the biggie.

You must allow yourself to see your dreams. That means you must open your mind up. You must get beyond your one-third brain power and just for a moment contemplate the viability of this truth. If you could just open yourself up to this truth and feed on it like manna, you would move through your day **dreaming** your way, **realizing** your way on the path that brings you joy.

What is it that makes you happy? Getting what you want. Correct? It is when you don't get what you want that you are unhappy. But people say to you, "Ahhh, 'tis better to give than to receive." So you put on the cloak called martyr.

When you are a martyr, you are not happy.

A dancing vivacious ecstasy of joy comes when you realize what you dream. And you simply do not appreciate a fulfillment to the same degree when it comes as a result of someone else's efforts. There is a much greater sense of joy when the fulfillment comes from acquiring the thing or doing the deed yourself. True?

You might really admire the first genius you meet. But then go on and meet a few more and the admiration pales. But I can assure you that if you were admiring your own genius, the rapture would be complete. Why is it so hard to give to yourself?

If you listened to this truth and learned, and did not take it out of context or hack it up, if you truly allowed it to be as original as I've given it, your dreams and the realization of freedom that is absolute would flow to you like a river. And your life in the time flow would speed up, because the period of manifestation quickens with every dream you manifest.

By the way, I still recommend you dream about freedom in the sense of freedom to dream, rather than financial freedom, because that doesn't really exist. If you think about who owns your money you must then take it to the next step and realize you could never be free while you're working on a loan. If you already figured that out, you may go to the head of the class, because that is pure reason, and that would indicate the lights are going on.

It is only with knowledge that you are going to be able to embrace this dream of freedom and bring it into fruition.

Do you want to know how to become the magician who goes on to become the Christ? You begin with a sincere hunger for knowledge of God and eternal life, and you take that hunger to the zenith. Sitting right where you are now, you can begin to understand these things in your own language, in your own way, and this truth can become a living truth to you. This is how you become the magician who becomes the Christ.

Why doesn't everyone **get** it? Because many of you are locked-in, attitude-wise, and you simply do not allow your attitude to give you up so that you may go forward. You still have your hands held high in the air, "Give me, give me, give me. I deserve for you to give to me. I don't really like myself, but I know I should get something anyway."

This is a paradox which only allows you to just survive. You never really arrive.

I can literally **hear** your process of comparing what you have read to what you thought to be truth regarding these issues. That's all right. There is plenty of room for you to grow. This truth is timeless. It will be here for all time because that is simply how the coagulation of thought into matter occurred—through emotion. You are the result of a dream that was realized. Your whole world is a dream realized! Don't you know that God is dreaming?

Evolution can only happen when the dream is realized in material form. And when the form begins to change, that is when the dream is realized, the dream of God, in which you become the main player. So this is timeless. There are many things happening in your social structure, but there is still no deadline on this understanding.

There is a wondrous woman out there thinking, "But I just

can't do it all by myself." You can certainly feel that way, as long as you know you have created the dream called helplessness.

And your dream of poverty will only deepen itself, because you cannot listen to this truth and know that it is a truth and then say you cannot do it. For then you only create lack! And it is all right to have that dream as long as you realize you are the one that is putting the block up.

This process ceases to be a game when you bring about your first manifestation. Dreaming is only a game when you're asleep and feel you have no control; that's when dreaming is a game from now on. But you create the slumber and you create the circumstances.

Let me tell you what freedom is. Freedom is manifesting a dream while bypassing gold.

Only when you know what you are, will you be happy. You have taken credit for your failures all your life. And you've handed a little blame around to your parents, your lover, the government, and even the dog next door. A little of everybody is to blame for this awful life of yours! But, by and large, you have taken credit for your failure and you have accepted your failure.

If you take the same energy and realize that you created the failure, you will realize it was a dream, and it's time to get beyond the dream. The moment you bring your own manifestation into focus, a wind will come from nowhere to laugh with you. That means you're home free.

*"Maybe it would have been easier to
just sit and meditate, but you've got to
do what makes sense to you. Seems I spend
a lot of my life convincing myself that
what I believe is really true."*

Trick of the Light

Embracing the Dream –
The Actual Process

The actual process of manifesting needs to be done sitting on the floor, or literally on the ground itself. You need be as close as possible to the magnetic field of your earth.

Even the bacteria that live in the earth know, through their own polarization, which direction is north, south, up, and down. They know through instinct. Their instinct is guided along the electromagnetic field. To create, you need to be as close to nature as you can get, for there, after all, is the most splendid example of a continuum continuing.

So, sit on the floor if you must, certainly not on a chair. Preferably sit on the earth. Additionally, sit so that you are aligned with north and south. This is to be done so that your auric field will blend quite nicely with the earth's electromagnetic fields, which vacillate from polar region to polar region and then swirl around the belt of Cancer.

Now, don't make this a ritual sort of thing in your mind. Rituals must always be secondary to knowledge.

If you put the ritual first, you have defeated the purpose you are trying to accomplish. You can sit here on the floor, aligned with north and south and the belt of Cancer, all day long, until you turn blue, and when you walk out the door, you can still be stupid. Well, I don't mean to be offensive, just humorous. Also, there is a great truth in that which must be communicated.

Your brain is a receiver that allows the thought to come in. It is only through pushing those buttons that the thought of God has a place to connect to. Through your brain, the thought is vacillated throughout your body and recorded in your soul. And it is with that knowledge recorded in the soul that you can perceive to work with future, present, past, future desire, emotion, and present body past.

So, you need to be on the floor to continue this process.

This is an individual experience, not something you all should meet on Saturday night to do collectively. You may be learning in a collective as a demonstration of understanding. But remember, great masters went out into the desert or did this on a walk. They sat under a tree or by a running brook or in front of a great deep. It doesn't matter, as long as it is on the earth. Not on the throne, but on the earth. You can gain this knowledge collectively. You can be outraged at this collectively. And you can laugh at my humor collectively, but go and be alone to work with this knowledge.

I will continue to direct you for group understanding, in case you are working in that format, but I will also address you individually, step-by-step. I strongly recommend that you work with this material privately, so that nothing gets in your way.

The ultimate trick is to put this information into practicality. Rituals are boring sorts of things. This is a **doing** that has knowledge behind it and a purpose in the silence between the words. Words are a limitation. In silence you are free to explore the realms of emotional truth, **emotionally**. Every single thing that is scientific is backed up with an emotional creativity.

What gave the atom motion? What gives the new wondrous quasar the breath of life to explode into the breath of life that creates universes?

Emotion. Everything you have done in all of life has been through emotion.

Except that your lives have been narrow-minded and your emotion has only been spit in the sphere of survival. Do you know how that one works? You find a lassie or a lad and you have great passion together. You have a few rolls in the hayloft. You can't live without one another. Who cares about tomorrow? Except that tomorrow comes and the hayloft is worn off, so you go find a better lad or lassie. "We need more money. I want a better house, a bigger buggy. And I need more clothes." You know. That's where your whole focus has been.

Learning, in silence, how to become emotional is the key that unlocks the kingdom of heaven, because pure emotion is pure truth.

How can you get emotional about something you are a hypocrite to? How can you get jazzed about something you don't want to be jazzed about? How can you get a thrill in helping another person, if that person makes you sick on the inside?

The point is, when you are in silence and learn how to embrace, you are not going to be lying to yourself. Right **in there, emotionally,** is where the dream lies. It is up to you to embrace it, emotionally, sitting there right now, like some great canary!

Do you think the **Thought** went around screaming all day? Do you think the original **Thought** went around chirping through lily fields, singing lullabies, thinking about creating it all? No! It just **was.**

I want you to learn to emotionally embrace the dream that you put down in script. You can't sit there and say the name of the dream over and over until it becomes a chant. That doesn't do anything, and you become hoarse to boot!

*I want you to become aware of being the
player in your own drama.*

You will **become** the dream. You will go within, and in a moment you will begin to embrace the dream by taking hold of it and living it vividly. In other words, in a moment you will become what it is you want, emotionally.

When you have learned to sidestep gold, you have a wild and free platform on which to create, because there is nothing inside of you saying, "But this is going to take a lot of money." And if you know better, and you still think that you need the money, you deserve to fall on your face, in the sense that you won't be able to bring the dream to recognition. If, however, you go with the dream emotionally and embrace it for the love, for the need, for the I AM, for the want that you desire, it **will** happen.

That which is embraced within the soul emotionally then goes back into time, distance, and space. It is lowered in frequency and becomes the reality called future and, indeed, destiny. That, my beloved masters, is how creation works.

If you think your life has been a bum rap all of these years, what about the bum that made it that way?

Well? Come on, you know the game you play. "Nothing's fair and I'm always the victim." You created it!

God doesn't say, "You're right and you're wrong." Nor does God say, "I shall exalt you while I choose to bring you down." God is life perpetual. God allows. God does not determine right or wrong. God just allows. That is called unconditional love, and you're not going to be able to turn around and look back into the face of God until you're happy. Only then will you know what you're looking at. See how simple this is? You can take this knowledge with you anywhere. You can take these tools of creation with you anywhere. If you're emotional, you've got the keys in your hand.

Look around you right now. Where are you? Look at the flooring or the carpet under you that isn't Persian. What about the light in your room? Smoke doesn't come off your lights anymore. It's all imitation—the greatest form of flattery. What about the design in your favorite rug? How do you think that design happened? Someone had an emotional insight. They took that emotional insight and drew it out on paper and said, "Look at this. Isn't this a wonderful design? Wouldn't it make a lovely carpet for a grand teacher to walk on one day?"

It all begins with an emotional insight. It is the same with electricity. Candles are obsolete now because someone had an idea, emotionally, and thus it became. There is not one thing in your home or one thing that you are wearing, even the way you cut and style your hair, that isn't emotional in its creation.

Reason this for yourself. The dream that is hanging over you, so to speak, is a limitation. It is unfulfilled, pregnant with possibility. What is it that brings it into manifestation? **Emotionally becoming the dream.** That is how you become God.

So the first step is knowledge, and the second step is the process of embracing, and that is where you go to work.

Have you heard the phrase, "Remove your shoes, for you are on holy ground?" That is not to protect the ground, but to allow the energy to be closer to you and to allow you the full benefit of what the ground has to offer you. So do it. Take off your shoes to engage this process. Consider your clothing, especially your waistband or anything that binds or constricts you. Remove your belt or anything that isn't loose, because if you're sitting there suffering you cannot go freely into the space of alignment. Nothing must bother you.

When you learn to do this, there is a reason that you should wear clothing that is very loose and speaks gently and softly to your body.

Remove all your jewelry. Did you know that it carries the vibration of the history of your relation to it? When you remove your jewelry, you remove your past. And when you remove your past, you are no longer allowing the jewelry to interfere with what you are ready to create in this now.

Many of you wonder why you cannot forget yesterday. You are haunted by your yesterdays. You have bad dreams about them. The moment you remove what binds you to them, you will no longer have the bad dreams. In manifestation, you should be as naked in energy as possible. That doesn't mean you have to take your clothes off, just your old energy and past histories.

Now, stop for a moment and feel the space where you are sitting. If you are sitting alongside other people in a collective experience of demonstration, consider whether you are sitting by a stuffy-shirted person. How do you feel where you are sitting?

Get in tune with it. If you are not feeling well in that spot, get up and move. If you feel stifled by anyone sitting near you, move to another spot. If that person takes offense, that's their dream. Get it? Do not do this elbow-to-elbow with anyone else either. As I said before, this process is preferably done alone.

What is important is that wherever you are, you must be comfortable and able to be alone emotionally with the dream inside.

Think for a moment about the dream you wrote down. What was it that you wrote down? Bring it back into your consciousness. Remember how the clarity felt when you wrote it down.

Now close your eyes and go into the principle of what is called the divine alignment to manifest.

Know what it is that you desire. Make it clear without confusion.

The state of desiring must be very clear. Speak from the Lord God of Your Being, for that brings forth what you call the future, to what is termed your present, to what is termed your past, and with that you will be aligned. In that moment of alignment, from the Lord God of Your Being, call forth the dream into power, into manifestation. It is up to you to do that.

Now, **have** the fantasy of becoming your dream emotionally.

What does that mean? It doesn't mean that you sit there and meditate! Meditation is a monotone prayer.

You must sit there with your eyes closed, so as to shut out the reality that looms out here and to allow you no restriction to the creativity within. You are not expected to sit there and contemplate God. You don't really know what God is yet.

I want you to become as involved with this fantasy as you do with your sexual fantasies. I want you to become **that** involved with this dream.

I want you to **become** the dream.

How will you know when you're there? When nothing else exists, save what you are feeling **inside**. When you are able to dream **inside** and become like a grand actor on the stage of life, playing the part in the preeminence of the profession by **becoming** it totally. You will know when this happens because nothing else will exist and a suspension will occur.

Your cardiovascular system will slow and your breathing will deepen. There will be a temperature change in the body. When there is a temperature change, there is a frequency change.

When all that exists, you are there.

You know you have created the dream when the laughter comes from the soul in the midst of a desired dream. When the joy is so lived that it becomes vocal and engulfs you, the dream is yours. In that moment, it leaves you. That is the orgasm of creation.

When the dream leaves you, you will feel weak. That is the moment it goes back into time and through the process to create and formulate your destiny.

And when you get through the rudimentary processes, there will come an hour when your movement leaves no footprints. A time when what you say becomes law in a moment. A time when what you feel **is**, when in a moment it **becomes**.

Miracles are the aftermath of creation.

And there will come an hour when you will no longer sit and embrace from the Lord God of Your Being, for you will **be** the Lord God of Your Being. Getting through the dream is what takes you there. And that is when you will walk as a Christ, when everything just **is** and the power walks with you.

Now, some of you will endeavor to do this, but you will stop in the middle and wonder what people would say if they could see you. And those of you working in groups will wonder what the person beside you is thinking and whether he is getting there faster than you. And some of you simply won't get anywhere because you are too worried about what you look like doing this. Think about this, if it helps: the person who's looking at the back of your head has someone looking at the back of his head.

And if you reach a moment of ecstasy and dare to shout out in the bliss of your emotion, and you stop and say, "What will they think of me?" you'll lose it. You will have to go back in and recreate it until you own it.

I understand there are some of you who just don't get this. It has gone completely over your head because you're too busy thinking, "Don't bother with this process, I'm only going to get what I've been getting." And so you will.

But those of you who desire to know freedom, this is how you'll get there.

Let's go for it!

Remember your dream. Bring it up.

Close your eyes. Breathe! Deeply! Create a new air!

Start with this prayer and then live the dream!

FROM THE LORD GOD OF MY BEING
UNTO THE FATHER WITHIN,
UNTO THIS HOUR,
COME FORTH
INTO ALIGNMENT;
COME FORTH
INTO POWER;
COME FORTH
INTO MANIFESTATION;
COME FORTH
INTO LAW.
UNTO THIS MOMENT,
UNTO THE FATHER WITHIN,
I GIVE THIS TESTAMENT
OF THAT WHICH I CREATE
TO THE GLORY OF GOD THE FATHER,
WHICH IS ALL
THE ALL
FOREVER
AND EVER
AND EVER.
SO BE IT!

Now, picture your dream. Embrace it. Live it. Own it. Allow it.

If you knew that by tomorrow everything you
desired would be yours, how would you feel?
It is with that intensity that you manifest!

What if I told you that your first dream would manifest to the intensity that you embraced it? I hope you comprehend that, because that is exactly how it will be! So be it!

Don't ask for the money to feed your family. Ask for the bread. This is a great teaching that embodies its own test. If you accept that your dream is a limitation and you accept that it can be realized, will you react?

Whatever you feel about that which you desire
is the feeling you are going to manifest in the
drama you create.

That is a biggie. Think about that for a while.

If you manifest your dream and then say, "Why don't I feel joy?" that is because you did not create it in joy. You may still manifest the dream but you'll wonder where the joy went. When your dream is embraced vividly, intently, and with the same emotion that you want to feel when it comes into fruition, then expect the same energy to manifest the same results.

Now that you know that, you want a second chance at manifesting, right?

It's a wonderful thing to hold a key that unlocks the door. The Kingdom of Heaven is truly one of possibilities and unlimited understanding. And when you realize that it is emotion which unlocks that door, I'll bet you'll **feel** this experience more vividly the next time you try it, hmmm?

To embrace that dream, you must live it as vividly as you wish it to be, because it is emotions that give governance and law to manifestation. That is as simply as it can be put.

So let's do it again **with feeling!**

If you're tired, go to bed. If you're hungry, eat. If you're ready to create your destiny, let's do it.

You know how to begin now. Play loud music if that helps shut out other intrusions into your space. Bring up the dream. Etch it in your mind. Cast the characters or watch them appear as you start the dream. Close your eyes. Be aware of your emotion in doing this. What do you want to feel when the dream comes true? Be vocal with this. There is no time in doing this; forget your concerns about time. You must embrace your dream, because in embracing, time doesn't exist. It is only when it is manifested that time comes into play. Go back and do it with intensity until you own it.

I love you people. Now, picture your dream. Light it up. Feel it.

When the dream has given you up and you feel done with it, say "So be it" with meaning and know you've owned it.

So be it.

Now, toast yourself with a glass of water with a small slice of lemon in it—the bitter water, I call it.

TO MIRACLES.

Call it forth:

FROM THE LORD GOD
OF MY BEING,
IT IS LAW.
SO BE IT.

"If the Truth was something that could be learned from a book, someone would have written it down long ago."

Trick of the Light

The Unlimited Truth Possesses No Words

How many words must issue from my mouth to bring you to the simplicity of all creative power? It is the emotion within you. What does it take? Are you so intellectual that you feed only upon the processes of words? Are you no more than a mathematician, so all things must add up?

I will do whatever it takes to get you to go within to the possibilities that lie there. The unlimited truth possesses no words, for if it can be spoken, it is a limitation. It is not what is said. It is not what I am saying. It is what I am not saying. That is the light.

What can I say to you to get you in touch with **you**, to get you inside to the emotion? What can I **say** to do that for you? There is nothing.

How do I say to you, touch the hem of your garment and feel the virtue of your own soul fall through? You must be in contact with **you**—no one else. That is the only way to realize where reality comes from.

You are Great Gods. You are humanoid entities that walk in light. Hear this: the voice of God is not the ringing forth of poetic words. It is the love. It is the emotion. It is the feeling. It resonates and rings with truth, if you touch it.

You are always emotional entities; that is what you are. And for good reason. Your body's greater physical makeup is aqueous substance. The soul and spirit's substance is emotion. And emotion is simply the Thought of God embraced into an emotional body, and the spirit and soul house the thought.

Light! Where do you think light came from? Light is the thought that contemplated itself and through contemplation bore emotion. Emotion is light.

What I haven't said is what you dare to feel. What is the great voice that cries in the wilderness? It is not another being talking to you, as many surmise. It is not your guides. It is not your teachers. Grow up!

The great voice that talks to you is the emotion in you.

It is the original thought being embraced. It is the seat of God's love through feeling. Emotion. That is what I cannot teach you. I cannot put it into words. I can only exude it to you.

It is what I don't say. It is what I feel for you. It is the wind, the runners to teach you, the knowingness, the feeling. That is the voice in the wilderness and that is what you ignore.

To become intellectual, you must become unemotional. You become godless and you never truly live.

Emotion. What is its fervor? It is the Holy Spirit. It is the Holy Ghost. When you touch the fervor of emotion, you are in alignment with the Holy Ghost. What is the Holy Ghost? It is the spirit of your being. It is connectedness with the inner light.

Don't you know that everything which surrounds you was made through the emotional embrace of idealism? Everything. Your clothes, your cars, your fads. Everything around you. How can you open your eyes and see the Creator and dare not feel emotion?

What do you say about your neighbor? Judge him not! Leave him alone. Allow him. And so what if the whole of the world throws stones at you? Allow them. As long as you hold your truth **inside**, you cannot be hurt. That's impeccable truth. Living your truth is emotion—it is power.

But do you do it? No. You quiver when the person next to you hollers out in the wilderness in great joy of being! They are living their dream. They are in the midst of a fire that's embraced. They are enacting the fantasy emotionally, and when they cry out, you snicker and laugh and blush. You are embarrassed for them! Woe to you! You are the godless, for without living the emotion there is no life.

For a decade the legacy has been, **"Behold God. The Father and you are one. The Kingdom of Heaven is within."** That is how you open up and perceive the world. That is law. And if your neighbor in this has seen the beauty of that and you see it as a bum rap, well, so it will be.

The words have never changed; only this ritual is a new thing.

Don't you know a cell **feels**? Don't you know a tree **feels**? It reaches for the light. It has a grand intelligence. Don't you know a rock **feels**? It has emotion. Without emotions, it would not be co-agulated thought turned into gross matter. That it **exists** proves it has emotion. Physics!

Everything is alive. Everything is a living organism. What determines life is emotion. And somehow, someway, it all came into a living, breathing organism. What loved it so much and embraced it so much to bring it forward? God the Father. Pure thought embraced!

You want to be rich? You want to have your own land? You want to have your own food storage? You want to **know**? You want to have a new car? A better job? You want to have fame? Glory? You want the means to survive? Preservation? So be it!

When you touch the emotional self, it creates it all.

And when you really understand that and begin to do it, you will live through that dream and come out to the other side very rapidly. You will own it all. And what would you fear? You will have stepped out of social consciousness, and would that be bad? Social consciousness is intellectual; it is not emotional. You would be out of the whining, the poverty, the misery, the hunger, the revolutionists who exist because of money, not because of themselves. There is nothing wrong with stepping out of social consciousness.

So if you have done that much, why haven't you got it all? Because you only took the teaching to the point that it glorified you or worked within your box! And the box is the system! You know the system. That's where you must amass gold so you can have the power to rule everyone else.

*Let me tell you what you are as long as you
are in social consciousness.*

You are the rabble in the street that is ruled. When you take this teaching and put it in the box that is the system, it doesn't work. But when you step outside the box and go around into your fulfillment of freedom, when you go around the oppressor, you have it all!

*The only way you can get it without buying it
is to feel it. Then you own it.*

Then it comes from many sources. There will be many runners. Many doors will open and many opportunities will come, and all of them will be grand.

God is not somber. It doesn't mean that God is grim just because neither the purple sky at midnight nor the silver crescent that hangs there speaks directly to you. Why, joy holds the very sky up! If it weren't for joy, there wouldn't be anything in the sky. It is life. Every star at midnight is joy, because it is through joy that it has life.

What is the life? It is the gasses that explode and come together and give the stars the friction to be, and it is the love and the joy that set them there.

God is not somber. God is rolling thunder. Laughter. Joy.

If you approach manifestation in somberness, you will lose it, unless you want to have one drag of a miracle happen! Get the point?

You are so close to the understanding of all these words that you can touch it now. If the knowledge comes to you and you own the knowledge that money is not yours because you aren't the one who issued it, because it's someone else's paper, if you are clear on that, then you **own** the knowledge! And if you can feel it, if you are an emotional being and you can take that knowledge into emotion, then you own it all. All of it.

Don't ask for the money to feed your family. Ask for the bread. And when you get the bread, say, "I am filled." Do you understand? So it becomes law.

You see, when you say, "I want to know; I earnestly do," and your words match your emotion, then it is so. Then you learn. Then I can teach you. Then I can bring you to a point where it all falls into place. And you can walk away free. **"I AM. I AM. The Father within me and I are One."** That's the whole purpose of this.

*"If I could give you anything, it would
be an ability to think of nothing . . . to simply
perceive the truth **directly** without 'thinking'
it out of sight."*
*"But it all seems so strange—this idea of
the world being an illusion that I should try
to make go away."*
*"The 'illusion' is like a fabulous magic
trick.*
*"It's the Light of God shined through
a prism of our beliefs and fears, then broken
up, bent and shaped into all the lines, colors,
shades, patterns, sounds and smells of the
physical universe.*
*"The Light is the only thing that is real.
The rest is just . . . a trick of the Light."*

Trick of the Light

The Trick Is
to Teach You to Own It

The world will never understand me because the world, as it is now, vacillates toward the negative.

The world will never never understand the sovereignty of an entity, because the world is owned. The world will never know God and understand the individualism of self, the living organism of the earth, because your world is bought and paid for, for at least a lifetime.

But I am here to teach you how to be sovereign. Are you going to say, "But it is unorthodox. It is embarrassing!"? Would you rather be embarrassed or be hungry? Take your pick. If it is unorthodox, it is unlimited.

The trick is to teach you how to own it, so that you can be a light unto your world; so that you know what it is to say, "God and I are One and the same," and have it mean something. If you own it, you can live out the days that are coming in your future in the peace and tranquility that passes all understanding. If you own it, you will see the meek inherit the kingdom that is left over from the tyrants. And if you own it, you will have the genius to create anew.

But unless you are emotional, you will never own that genius.

Where do you think the great new minds will come from? **You**.

As unorthodox as you are and as outrageous as I am, this works. Emotion and feeling.

You have been sitting there reading this information. If you joined along and followed my direction, you have had a jolly toast. You don't necessarily remember the words, but it was jolly, nonetheless. Something about "To Life, and from God" and all that. You've read a lot of things that made sense. I said a dirty word or two and you snickered. (They're not dirty. An ass is an ass! It is a living thing.)

You have listened and some things have caught your attention and made you want to know more. And that brain of yours has begun to think; it has come out of mothballs. And if you moved to the floor and genuinely expected something great to happen, well, it did. Indeed!

You can't say, "From the Lord God of My Being," and then say, "What did I say?" You can't say, "From the Lord God of My Being, would you give me a loan?" That's a jolly hypocrisy.

Make it happen! Make it happen.

Making the Miracle Happen

Now, remember that I said your desire is in the future, your emotion is now, and your body is in the past? Well, that leaves a lot of you running around with old bodies that feel quite young. You see, your bodies are responding to your acceptance of an attitude that that's how they are supposed to be. You made them that way. In other words, you have expected to age so you have aged.

Everything lags in the physical. Let's reason this out. You have taken the dream, which lies **out there someplace**, tenuous and in the future, and brought it **in here**, inside you. And you have taken the emotional self—which is the forever now—and embraced it in the body. And the body that yelled, quivered, sweated, breathed deeply, wept, cried out, felt, and clapped was the body of the past.

It is a matter of conceptualizing what you call time. That is the thing that has to play catch-up in order to make a miracle happen.

But when the body becomes involved through the process of manifestation, it is pure alignment the moment it becomes the **now** absolutely. Everything is in focus then. When you manifest like a person with a fantasy for copulation, the body responds in a moment. It is a miracle. It is a manifestation of an emotion.

It is when your body actually responds to the joy that the dream leaves you. It must manifest into time to become coagulated, so that tomorrow the destiny of your very time begins to change automatically. Then you know you have won.

In the Flow of Time

Sitting and meditating doesn't make it happen. It gets you in touch all right. You know you are alive; you are breathing; you are sitting down and you are meditating. It does bring peace, because if you desire peace in meditation, you get it. But manifestation is emotion—pure emotion. And if you just sit there and through your orthodoxy simply say, "I own it, it's mine, so be it," it isn't going to happen. You are going to cry out incredulously and say, "Why didn't it happen? This doesn't work." Well, if it doesn't work, how do you justify your brother's genius coming into bloom? It **has** to be the body, mind, spirit, and soul together.

Let's look closer at your concept of time: $E=mc2$. Let me tell you how time started.

Any moment you move off of **now**, you are in a time flow. When light first moved away from the thought, time began, because when the light moved away from the thought, it began to slow down. And as it slowed down, its frequency slowed until it became the coagulation of gross matter.

It takes time for what you create to leave you and to **fall**, so to speak, through time into coagulated matter. Every moment that emotion slows down, it quickens itself into matter. That is the law of mathematics. And that is what sets up your destiny that is called your future. I will tell you this. There is one thing that you know for certain. Your future does exist, if for no other reason but for the dream that you manifested this day. By law, it must occur! So be it.

Well, how else are you going to tell me that next year is coming? Are you going to show me a calendar? Spare me. Are you going to tell me, "Because that is when my birthday is?"

The future cannot be scientifically proven. The future is pure conjecture. What makes it absolute is destiny ordained. And your manifestation of the dream has ordained it, for certain, and it is already in the process of becoming.

If you look at your calendar, it will tell you the year. And there may even be pictures there to assure you that winter will indeed come. Other than that, there is no way for you to know that the future exists. But when you take control emotionally, everything that you direct intentionally must come. That is how your future is sustained.

You should drink to that.

TO NOW,
FOREVER
AND EVER
AND EVER.
SO BE IT.

You've Been Going Around the Corner in Your Same Old Box

Now that you understand emotion better, let's go back to the process. Remember your first dream? Now you own it. But what did you do with the second thing on your list? Is there one? Or did you write your first dream to encompass everything you ever wanted? If you did, you gypped yourself. What will human nature do when you have created all your dreams? You will create another one, of course. It's called evolution.

*Some of you are under what I call **limited thought**. You really think it can't happen, so it doesn't happen.*

There are some of you who sit and align and do all this kind of stuff, but when you open your eyes and look in the mirror, you see the same old puss. Nothing has happened. You sit there and you wish and you dream and you embrace emotionally and you even feel like you are walking on a fluffy cloud. And you just **know** it's going to get better—except when nothing has gotten better in half an hour, you say, "This stuff doesn't work."

Do you know why it doesn't work for you? Because ignorance

is rampant. Everything you have learned on this plane has been a gross limitation, because no one on this plane ever knew the truth of how it really worked. You have only gotten rituals. And what did you get for understanding only half the truth? You got fragments of long periods of suffering, celibacy, fasting, chanting, guides, ghosts, ectoplasm, teachers, channels (real and unreal), and books. Great titles, too: *How to Become God in 30 Days. The Joy of Leaving Your Body*, by I Am Gone.

Do you see why there has been so much garbage? Everything you valued in your material world was created by amassing gold, which led to the power to enslave. No one knew any better because they lived in that consciousness. Don't you see? Bring it home, inside, **that is where the truth belongs.**

If you are sovereign, then no one owns you anymore. But if you are without dignity, and you are not a royalist, and you have class problems, you can be owned, manipulated, and fooled for greater purposes that don't extend beyond this earth.

Getting new information means you have to look at everything you have catalogued. "Oh, I can't do this. I don't have the insight. Some people are born with it, but not me. I suppose there's a lot to be said about karma."

Karma is a limitation. It is a sexist limitation. It is a class limitation. It exalts some and destroys others. It doesn't exist.

Tidbits have been thrown out to you, and you've gobbled them up. You grapple with them, but they don't work. Yet you tell your friends that your life changed as a result of your newest understanding. Well, I'd be ashamed to take such a compliment, because what did you change into? You've just been going around the corner in your same old box. You are just seeing the room from a different perspective.

No one got the whole picture, because it was too simple.

Do you know that in a twinkling of an eye you can own it?

*"But my experience has been that present time is like a funnel in that as you approach it, it appears to get smaller and smaller; so that there appears to be just a pinhole opening of light at the far end. Yet the closer you get to the tiny funnel opening, the wider the hole of light starts to appear, until finally, when you reach the opening, you realize that the funnel was just a gateway into the infinite now—a magic moment that is not only greater than the past or future, but, in fact, **contains them both.**"*

Trick of the Light

To Be the Dream

You need rudimentary knowledge to help you understand science and mathematics.

Time is based on the speed of light. The velocity of light moving from one distance to another determines time. What you create when you manifest this way has to go from the ethereal, emotional body to become destiny, which then comes into a time flow out beyond you, and then spirals in, so that it becomes, so that it happens.

But where is the joy? You have just set yourself up for it.

Patience is a virtue. Hold onto patience and understand time. Each time a dream comes to you, you will go into another, and you will find yourself glad and joyous. You will love yourself better, because there is something happening. You become aware of your creation. You are worth it! God really does think you are terrific.

Each time you manifest, you will go on to the next one and then the next. You will find that you are transcending, you are eliminating, you are owning all the limitations. You are mastering.

Don't you know that mastery is to master the dream? It is not to suppress the dream. It is to **be** the dream. That is how you clear out the decks to be the Christ. The more that you embrace, the closer you get, the more powerful you become, and in a moment, it is so, because you are no longer a hypocrite to your words and your emotions.

Your emotions **are** the truth. That is what is impeccable. Learn to say, "I will not compromise. It isn't in me to compromise. I AM what I AM. What I say I AM, and to the God of My Being, I am pure emotion back into the thought."

To be a hypocrite to your emotions is to live a duality, and that leads to lies that breed sadness and confusion. What is confusion? It is the reflection of the dual self in **here**—inside you. A hypocrite is one who says one thing and is another emotionally. Be impeccable. After all, what judgment from the world is worth holding you away from the impeccability that will take you back to the light? What do you care of the world and its attitude?

> *To love the world and allow the world is grace, and that is impeccable, but to be who you are, is God.*

This is not about martyrdom. It is about changing your values. What value can you put on knowing how to create? What value can you put on knowing how to recreate? How to gain the light? How to be powerful? Or how to be God? That demands impeccability.

My daughter has learned a hard thing. She is impeccable to her dreams. She has learned to be what she is in this embrace.

In this dream of yours to be free, live what you are **inside**, not what someone tells you you are. Have the patience to understand and the genius to know the science of things, and everything you ever wanted, everything that has kept you turning on the wheel of life, everything that you lust for, hunger for, and need, you will have.

It is called the path of joy. It is what takes you home. Be patient. Own what you have learned today. Don't talk about it to other people. Be impeccable with your emotions. The moment you start comparing what you embraced with someone else, you wonder if you asked for enough, or perhaps if you asked for too much. And you know how people are when you have too much. They don't like you. Ask my daughter!

Own it. Carry it all the way through, as if it were the focal point of the magnet—that part which is neither positive nor negative. Own it. Carry it all the way into its fruition. And the moment it manifests, you can tell the world about it.

I am endeavoring to move you out of narrow-mindedness, through pure reason, into absolute unlimitedness. And one way to get there is to have your own opinion and no one else's. And how do you do that? You never ask anyone what they think!

And when you can do that, a wind will come up out of nowhere to let you know that you did it; that you and the Father within have made this manifest; that it has become a reality to stand as a testament to you, a living symbol that God **is**. Then you can say, "Look! Look at this!"

Then you will know what I am saying about feeling joy. And then you are ready for the next dream and the next dream and the next dream.

You are like the fruit on the tree. There is a cluster of fuzzy-faced peaches and only one has the blush of the sun kissing its cheek. It falls from the limb only when it is ready. You are like that. You are falling from the tree. Be happy. Only when you get off the tree can you have a new life. So be it.

You are learning.

I ask this of you. When your dream has manifested and you are in your jubilance, from the Lord God of Your Being, thank the Father within. Give thanks to God. Don't forget that!

The Tomorrow That Never Comes

When you are busy talking or making a statement, you never listen. When you are allowed to ask a question, your mind races to find the right one, rather than to absorb the information you have just heard.

I have a few news flashes for you. I do not care about other entities. They all have their game. I care about you and what you learn. And what you can learn here definitely lies **outside** the box, and it is only within the box that games are perpetrated. There will never be another entity like me. There will never be another one like you. And what is important is the treasure within, not what lies in the narrow-mindedness of man. Is not the New Age an age of super-consciousness? If you keep looking at it as the New Age, it will continue to be the tomorrow that will never come. You can always postpone super-consciousness, super-power, super-manifestation, until tomorrow, if there is an excuse to do that.

The New Age is an illusionary future that never comes. And it never will. The reality of superconsciousness is here and now. It is a matter of resurrecting it and owning it.

I don't ask many questions anymore because you are too busy taking in the information. And the more you read and absorb, the more you learn; the more acutely you absorb what is not said. If you are busy lining up your questions, you will never become emotional enough to be powerful enough to own! Reason that out.

My daughter has grown very weary of this work, for many reasons. You'd get tired of having rocks thrown at you, too. You can be hit but so many times. But she is not tired of the learning.

I honor your desire for knowledge. It has taken great fortitude to undertake this tome from an entity that has been accused of condoning murder and the like! But like my daughter, you too, are not tired of learning, and believe me, there is another whole new frontier that opens up when you just get beyond the monkey-mind.

I allow my daughter her feelings, but I continue to tell her it is rolling over, for all that matters is what the Father within thinks and no one else. Don't ever get tired of wanting to learn. Do get tired of making yourself miserable. It only takes a moment to speak to the Father within you, to bring it forward. It only takes a moment to change your whole life. That is the legacy of this teaching.

You are going to have so much more than financial freedom. You are going to have much more than you even know exists, so that when you leave this plane and, nigh, you put your hands forward, they will be filled with riches of knowingness and wisdom. You will have your cakes and eat them too, many times over.

Once you know how to use the keys, you are in evolution, and you will evolve.

I love you. I know there are those of you who have cursed me and slandered me and hated me. I love you. You are still here learning, and that is because I never stopped loving you.

Be kind to you. Invest in you. This is enough learning for this passage. Go and have a hearty meal. Enjoy your brothers and have some festive times. Then go and find your peace and sit upon your sacred ground and do with fervor and gusto what you have learned here. Enjoy it. Go back to the Father within you. Pick your next realization, your next dream, your next limitation, and create. You know how to do it now. And if you have absorbed well, you will do it with pure emotion, and your body will pulsate and undulate from it all at once. Go and do it alone. And you will have as much power wherever as you have **inside**. Live what you have learned and be a living truth. One day you will be glad you did, for all the gold in the world will not be able to buy what you know. Impeccability. That is the greatest investment you will ever make.

And what does it take? Time. Solitude. Thick walls so no one will hear you cry out in the moment of your ecstasy.

Practice this until you become a pro at it. In the next passage, we will learn to go further than the dreams of limitations. So be it.

"If you're going to change your life, you must first change the way you perceive life."

Trick of the Light

On Having Your Cakes and Eating Them, Too!

I recommend a toast of bitter water before we continue. This prayer speaks to where we are in the journey you are now creating.

FROM THE LORD GOD OF MY BEING
UNTO THE FATHER WITHIN
UNTO THIS HOUR
COME FORTH
INTO ALIGNMENT
INTO KNOWING
INTO POWER
FROM THE LORD GOD OF MY BEING
UNTO THE FATHER WITHIN
THAT WHICH IS THE FUTURE
THAT WHICH IS THE NOW
THAT WHICH IS THE PAST
COME FORTH
INTO THE NOW
FOREVER AND EVER AND EVER.
SO BE IT.

The Man Who Dreamed the Dream of Thirst

Once there was a man who lay upon a pallet in his hovel, very near a window. The pane of this window had been cleansed so well that it gave the illusion that there was no force which prevented you from putting your arm through it and feeling the air.

And as this man slept on his pallet, he had a dream. In the dream, he was thirsty. And the pallet became the parched earth, and any movement caused the saffron dust around him to rise and then settle and thicken, in and among his eyelashes. And his tongue became swollen from thirst and his lips cracked from continuous licking until there was no moisture left.

And the dream was of profound thirst.

He lay on his pallet, which in his dream was the saffron-covered earth. And as he lay there, the sun, Ra, beat down unmercifully on him in its great zenith. He couldn't lift an arm or call out for someone to share just a drop of precious liquid to quench his thirst. And he rolled not on his pallet, lest he make the earth cake further on him. In this dream of his, he did not know he was dreaming, and he was sorely thirsty.

And as he lay there in torment, his lips and tongue unquenched, a gentle rain fell outside his window.

The Man Who Dreamed the Dream of Death

There was a man who lay on his pallet and dreamed a dream of fear. He dreamed a dream of dying. In this dream, he endeavored to run and outdistance the horseman, whose hooves he could hear in the far distance. But try as he may, he could not move, and he could hear the hooves coming closer and closer.

Desperately he called out to stay alive, but he could not move in his dream, and the horse's hooves struck fire on distant rocks and made the earth tremble. His heart was filled with panic, and he dreamed the dream of dying just moments away.

In this desperation to run, he did not notice the sun above or the wind in his hair. He noticed not the earth, the sweet earth, underneath his feet. And as he dreamed the dream of death riding closer and closer, outside his window the winter was turning into spring, and the nakedness of the great oak and its long sinuous fingers of barren limbs were budding the hope of spring.

The Man Who Dreamed the Dream of Lack

There was a man who lay upon his pallet and dreamed the

dream of poverty. In this dream, opportunity never came. In this dream of poverty, he was a beggar who took handouts in desperation. He had only one linen cloak, which had been patched numerous times, and his boots had no heels. And he had not one singular gold trinket that burnished and shone brilliantly in the sun. He had not one thing. This was his dream of poverty. And as he dreamed the dream, outside of his window, a gentle wind blew. The wildflowers bathed themselves in the sun, and the wind blew pollen and seeds to the earth's waiting uterus in harmony, balance and simplicity.

The Man Who Dreamed the Dream of God

There was a man who dreamed a dream that he was a God. In the dream, all things were possible. If he desired, in a moment he could go into the great deep and cast forth his net and bring up large fishes—meaty, shining, silver, opulent. When he cast his net, an abundance came forth from the sea.

In his dream that he was God, nothing in his sight ever died, and in this dream, the onslaught of seasons did not peril him. He dreamed a dream of joy, and all things resounded in music that was never off-key. It could be flat or sharp at different times, but it was always harmonious. In his dream, everything was vibrant, and hues of color extended beyond awakened senses. In this dream everything blended and created the song that is the thought of God.

And in this dream, he walked upon emerald meadows and saw flowers shimmering with the goldenness of their petals. Nowhere in his dream was there any anger, or malice, or judgement, or envy. Nor was there sickness, or pain, or sorrow. All was a forever that sang a song of harmony.

Thus was the man who dreamed the dream of God. Nowhere in his dream did he contemplate if he were dreaming, and he woke up to realize he was asleep.

Be the One Who Dreams the Dream of Waking Up

The dream that you live in is the dream.

When you awaken, it has nothing to do with what you see

around you. Because outside of the dream lies the harmonious possibilities of eternal life. Forever. And ever. And ever.

You are in a dream. And all of your perceptions, and even how you view your perceptions, are based on fallible things, not eternal things. You dream the dream that hides all other dreams.

You dream impossibility. And because that dream is the caretaker of all things unfulfilled, you live in the illusion of limitation.

Don't you know that outside your window it is raining?

Don't you know that outside your window what has died in the winter is being reborn in the spring?

Don't you know that what lies outside your window is the abundance of propagation? The seeds of genius?

Don't you know that you are asleep, dreaming of harmony? Dreaming of God?

Manifestation—what you are learning here—is the emotional science. It is the emotion that is awake. Your logic is dead. It is the emotion that is the vitality which transcends the horrors of intellect. Don't you know that when you are in the intellect, you have never lived?

When you are in the throes of manifestation, don't you know you are the god who walks in pastures of green grass and hears the song of harmony? For therein lies the forever that has neither the beginning nor the ending of such boundaries that limit the possibility of all things.

Evolution could not occur in nature if there were an ending. You, who tapped the power, see it in reverse. You see flagrant imagination and the ecstasy of a fantasy as unreal. It is the opposite. It is in the flagrance of emotional embodiment aligned that you create what is truly real from the Lord God of Your Being.

You think it is the opposite because that is the human drama.

The human drama ceases when it realizes the difference between illusion and reality. If you think that what you embrace when you go inside and bring forth the dream is flagrant imagination, then you must conclude that it is also flagrant imagination that the Kingdom of Heaven is within.

You have to know this. It has to ring with truth. For if the Kingdom of Heaven is within, it is the **within** that creates all of the **without**.

It is the **within** that garnishees you from the privilege of unlimited life and holds you in the narrow-mindedness of struggle. Do you know why you struggle? Because you are narrow-minded. Because you are asleep in a dream that you can't move in. When you wake up emotionally, all the struggle, all the sorrow, all the pain, all the hurt ceases.

When you wake up emotionally, it becomes harmonious. You are having difficulty possessing the honor to know. It is a privilege to know what you are learning. You are learning that you have to change your attitude about what is real and what is illusionary.

If you want to be a realist, be it in emotion, for there is no hypocrisy in that.

If you surmise and broaden your ability to reason to that place of pure reasoning, where you give birth to another part of your brain that allows you to embrace the majesty of a greater thought, you will innately know that what I have just said is a great truth. Your brain will open and allow you divine thoughts that are thoughts of God, not thoughts of the human drama. And in that thought, in that surmising, you will begin to realize that, emotionally, you created all your unhappiness, and it manifested in your dream of limitation.

And in a moment, in the midst of chaos, with a change of attitude, fired with desire, you can resolve it, own it, and become joyful, for there is no longer the chaos. I say unto you, this flesh and blood is going to pass, and it is the quality of the endowment of your spirit and of your soul that will supersede the kingdom of flesh and blood. It is only through that spirit and soul that the immortality of love, joy, and profound wisdom are sustained, for all other things fall away and the body goes back to the worm.

What is real? What sustains forever? By reasoning, one has to conclude that it is the kingdom: by taking the legacy of truth that **I AM GOD** to its zenith; by realizing that the perpetuality of what you are, is forever. **YOU ARE GOD.**

And what is it that you amass which is forever? The understanding that emotion is truth. Seeing the world through the emotion **within** is how you garner the riches called wisdom and the knowingness that creates a magnificent Light Being who wears victory over death, who wears victory over all the chains that bind you to the flesh. Forever and ever and ever.

You can't be a "realist" and know innately that you are forever. You know only that you are a hypocrite, the godless who never lived. To know, with the **emotions,** that you embraced the dream is the great reality, and to **absolutely** know that, is to be delivered from the dream, to wake up.

What is the light of God? What is the power of a Christ? What is the magic that escapes you completely? It is **emotional** truth. When it surfaces, you carve it up into portions and discard what isn't real in your dream.

Wake up! It's raining outside.

Wake up! Winter is passing. Spring's mauve and pink buds are on the sinuous black fingers of the mighty oak. It is living again!

Sweet Masters, to manifest is only part of the King's pie. For, you see, the King takes all of the pie. That is why he is the King! This embrace is only a part. You're dreamers who linger in the greatest limitation of all, the notion of impossibility.

What is guarded by impossibility can never be realized.

And thus you are not genius; you are the godless, the living dead, for you cannot realize what lies within that needs to be fulfilled. And why does it need to be fulfilled? Not to be an asset to mankind. Not to make nature happier with you. Not to line your pockets with gold. But, in essence, so that it can stand as a magnificent three-dimensional tribute to the power that lies within the glory of God the Father, forever and ever and ever.

It's not the gold. It is the magic of what is in it. It says, "Look at me. I came from the one who sent me." And unto that, His name is Forever.

It's raining outside, you who need money! And when it is spent, you will only need more.

Spring is coming.

Part of the pie is the ability to look at your freedom and feel that you are financially situated so that you can dedicate your life to God, right? No! You would only be continuously protecting your finances so that the bottom line balances.

You are still learning what is part of the pie. But that won't happen until your attitude is with it. Your attitude is turned against you right now, because, you see, this is all still just a delicious fantasy to you. The moment you put this book down and lie down in bed, you contemplate with your realistic mind: "This can't happen. I'm not worth it."

To change your attitude, you must use pure reason to the zenith of your character. You must release your monkey-mind.

How do you know how to open up the great seventh seal, the pituitary, the guardian of the seat of the brain? How do you open it up? If you try to do it through drugs, you'll die. If you try to do it through chanting, you'll grow hoarse. If you try to do it through meditation, you'll only run around and around the corners of your box. You get there by poignantly reversing the attitude, and then from that you begin to question the other side of the attitude.

What is real and what is illusion? Go on and ask, "What if? What if?" Take it beyond death; keep asking and the pituitary begins to respond. That wondrous brilliant elixir of hormones will begin to open up the brain and the pituitary will bloom like a great lotus. And the "what ifs" keep taking you further by opening the brain more and more, so that the thought, the beauty of what God is, can be embraced for all the depths of its mystery. That is what opens the great seal.

Lazy minds, metaphysical minds, spiritual teachers, diets, crystals, amulets, and zircons only adorn the box. They don't do anything else. You are still going to die, adorned. It isn't **outside**; it is **inside**. You are the greatest machine that was ever made. You are the living temple of the living God, and He lies there behind the dreams. And genius lies where the attitude is turned around.

Social consciousness is illusion. Emotion is reality. And if you could embrace that, you would quickly eliminate the caretaker of all the dreams, and they would begin to open and flow like a river. Where do they go? Back to God! You could look upon the surface of your dreams, like a river, and see your face. You could look in it and say, "'Tis I." Then you know. Then you possess knowingness. Then you possess the truth that transcends the idiocy of ritual. Then you possess the truth that extends beyond the game, beyond the box. It is the truth that extends all the way to immortality.

You are all capable of genius. It's not something I can give you, not something I can put in your hand. No runner will come bearing the gift of genius so that you may adorn yourself with it. It is not something that you will garner by languishing at the feet of another, hoping it will rub off on you.

It is innately already yours. Genius is the untapped resource, the brilliance, the quantum leap of a life that can extend into forever.

The body is controlled by the pituitary. The pituitary, through its hormone flow, sets up the gland that either induces life or prepares to end it.

You have owned a little bit of emotion that you reversed in your fantasy, but you do not own genius yet. Until you reverse emotion, the next step in manifestation will always leave you wondering and dismissing the process.

The Greatest Limitation of All Is Attitude

The greatest limitation of all is attitude.

Do you know why you never fully get it? Because **getting** it, to you, is a dream, and you dream that very few **get** it. Very few own it; are it; become it; demonstrate it. Your mind and your emotion are the greatest assets you can ever possess. They can never be sold. Man can take the body, but he can never take the soul, your spirit. He can throw stones at you, but he will never really hurt you. He can never bruise the soul and the spirit that is God. It forgives with compassion and lives on and on and on.

Very few will own this pie completely, because your monkey-mind rationalizes, "This is just the Ram's teachings." And many people have denied me and think I no longer exist, because when they decide I no longer exist, it makes it easier for them to dismiss what has been taught, and they no longer feel obligated to go to the next step. Do you see? I became their excuse. "It doesn't matter. It isn't real."

In manifestation, you'll get your great miracle and you'll wonder why you're still unhappy. You'll be jazzed in the moment, drinking your success to the rooftops, but then the next thing occurs and you forget all about what you just learned. Why? Because the attitude behind your manifestations is one of trepidation.

You say you sit quietly to engage this process of manifestation for fear of disturbing a neighbor. Oh, meek entity, the real reason you sit so quietly is because you have doubt about what you are doing.

If I gave you an amulet and said, "Go and rub this every night; soak it in water and take it out and drink the water," you would do it lickety-split! (And it would bring about some results.) But when it comes to **you,** all alone, you excuse yourself from participation by contemplating the attitude of reversal. "This isn't real." That's why some of you are healed in a moment from this teaching and others stay crippled.

Why do miracles happen to some and not to others who pray the same prayer?

Where is the attitude? That is all there is to it. The dream that holds you back, that keeps you from getting where you want to be, is a dream of your creation. You embraced it. The whole of society stands as immutable proof that you are right in creating it! Why, society tells you every day what is real. Every day it assures you through the murk and mire of the marketplace; through the wickedness of limitation. Man slanders and slays his brother and rapes innocence. Man negotiates and builds walls. Prices are in a flux and you are wondering where you belong in all of this. That is where you get the credibility that your old dream is real!

How do I wake you from that dream? You begin by contemplating this knowledge; that is where it starts to take shape. Knowledge, not ritual, engenders the growth of the brain. It changes the quality of life.

What can I do to break it down further? I can send many runners but, you see, they are only like a placebo. They can tell you, for a moment, that you are well, but then you get right back into your syndromes—right back into hate and anger, envy and bitterness, revenge, despotism, gossip, and even war. So runners have been only placebos. I cannot break down that attitude.

I can only feed you the knowledge and encourage you to reason every word. This will achieve an emotional impact, thus opening the brain. So, little by little, the lights will go on, and then you can say, "From the Lord God of My Being, I did it! The pie is mine!"

So what have I given you? What is my legacy?

A profound truth.

It is a matter of attitude turned inward that takes you to forever and ever and ever.

Reason it. What if? What if? What if? Add it up mathematically. Emote it. Contemplate it.

Everything you have ever done, you did because you wanted to do it. That, in and of itself, was a desire from emotion. Want is emotion.

And what is emotion? It is unseen power.

Then what transcends it?

It's raining outside. This is not new truth? This is forgotten truth.

Don't you know what lies on the other side? Reality.

What made you pick up this book? A feeling? And what else did you add along to that feeling? That, somehow, this book would teach you how to make yourself rich. That was your attitude.

But what was the spontaneity in the soul? Emotion. **Emotion.**

I say to you that those who live in the real world, those who are dreamers, are dead. They have worshipped the intellect and abandoned their emotion, relegating the concept of emotion to the foolish old women and the immaturity of children.

They have never lived.

And one day, they will have to eat their own words, for they will have no other substance.

Where are the mysteries? There aren't any.

*"No time like the present," I chimed in,
sensing the futility of voicing any objections.
Max got a sly look on his face and said,
"There is no time but the present."*

Trick of the Light

Life and Illusion

What are the mystery schools? You are in one. What is it that cannot be written down and must be hidden away? There is nothing. Superstition is like a faceless rider; it doesn't exist.

When you don't understand something, be suspicious of it. You know it all. You know it through **emotion**. It is emotion that fires the light. It is emotion that allows knowledge.

You are the hidden books. You buried them in fantastic illusion.

I know that if you were following along with the process in the order it is given here, you sat there the first time and meekly toyed with your dream. Then, when I told you your dream would manifest according to how you sat and embraced it, you wanted another chance. Why? Because something pushed a button and said to you, "I only receive what I create, and in the joy and the fathom of release, **I feel.**"

So you went back and began to **feel** a little bit more. Understanding that you work that way, I should have told you to act as if you'd just won a million dollars!

But I understand money. You don't. It's not your money! And someone is going to call the loan due. But in your reverse attitude, that would have made the difference.

I have talked about and have given you a profound teaching on the secret of all life, if you can embrace it.

It's raining outside, dreamers. But I know that if you can rationalize and reason for a moment,

*you will see that it is the **attitude** in which you embrace that distinguishes life from illusion.*

And with that clarity, you will be richly endowed to go on your path of joy.

Manifest all your dreams with an incredibly wise and prudent understanding that transcends the ignoble mind of common man.

The pie?

Manifestation is but a wee sliver of it.

Doing Destiny

To continue, it is necessary for you to understand destiny.

If emotion has created it—and by the law, it will—what is the next step required for destiny to match the emotion of the dream? You must be a doer. Doer. **Doer!** If you sit there with your mouth hanging and your hands open, you will miss destiny.

You have to get up and walk forward into destiny.

Genius has nothing to do with embracing a dream. As long as it is within you, it is not genius, it is a limitation. Genius is when the dream manifests and you embrace it in the physical. You are going to need to do that until you have clarified all your dreams, until one day you can sit in sackcloth and desire no thing of this plane except to bathe in the warmth of the morning light.

Only when all your dreams are finished can you sit on the throne of Christ.

My kingdom is not of this world, because I own it all. And you can sit there in sackcloth and say that all day and it won't matter, because you already dreamed the dream of a cloth of gold, and so it must be.

What is at the end of this path of enlightenment? To become **God/Man**, that God may see his face for the first time, and his incredible journey, called Himself.

Your kingdom will not be of this world, but of the world within: to own it all and not be wanton. That's why you need your dreams. But you can't have your dreams, you can't sit and bathe yourself in the light and leave no footprints as a Christ, until you have walked forward into your destiny. You have eloquently begun the creation of your new destiny. You may have laughed in peals and cried rivers of release in joyful freedom, and your soul may have felt immaculately clean on the inside, like a new garment, but you must **follow through**.

The next piece of the pie is to walk into the destiny you have created so that you can feel, touch, smell, and wear the dream, for the soul is already cloaked in its dream.

And then you must move on to the next dream and the next one. And on and on.

Doers are the geniuses. What makes a genius? The application of the dream! You could sit there all day and spout eloquent philosophies and have brilliant ideas, but your audience will leave you when their bellies start to rumble. They won't hear you any longer. They'll go off and eat and pick their teeth and wonder what a silly fool you are. You will impress no one, because, alas, they will see you as only a fool.

Doing is living. It you sit in your cave and think that God owes you something because you've realized all of this, the sun will never shine inside your cave. It will still be dark and damp, and your arthritic bones will ache.

Life is the gift to wake up into! It is the reality. Genius is the **doing**. The doors will manifest, but you must walk through them.

Do you think the gold bricks will fall from heaven? Fool!

Do you think you can just open your mouth and manna will come and fill you? Wake up!

Dreamers, it is only when you get up off of your bed, go open your window, stick your head out, and open your mouth that the rain can quench your thirst! It's raining outside.

Life is the gift to wake up into. It is the reality.

It is when you wake up that you no longer hear the flaming hooves of death. Then all you hear is the wind that rustles through the naked budded branches of spring. It is life. **LIFE**. Life shows you innately, "I am living again. I am resurrected from the winter. I am here again."

Wake up! Go and embrace the tree. Spring's coming. You're alive. Wake up from poverty. Get up and go out the door and sit in the meadow and let the pollen coat your face with abundance.

It's happening. The seeds are dreams blowing in the wind. They will implant themselves in the fertile uterus of the great Mother Earth, and they will rise up and bloom. They **get up** and

do. You dreamers who lie about in the dream and dream forever of chasing your tails in bad relationships, of being unhappy, of being victimized by your own creation, your dream is being victimized. You are continuously pursued into the depths of the muck and the mire of sorrow, and you wallow in it. You walk around and around in a box of your own dream of unhappiness.

Wake up! Go outside! There is a band marching by. Join it! You are lying on your pallet, dreaming every dream of yours. You are dreaming every dream you wish to escape from. They are haunting you around every corner.

You spiritualists! You hypocrites! You, who think that you own God and the truth and the path and the way and the light, wake up! All you are is a hypocrite, and you will die a frustrated entity. You are godless. Wake up and watch the dawn come. It will tell you everything you ever wanted to know.

Don't be afraid to cry in the wind or to hold a child and hear its heart beating in your chest.

Don't be afraid to pick flowers in the meadow and linger in their sweet perfume.

Don't be afraid to look in wonder at the purple midnight and the wondrous pale moon. And do be aware of the sinuous path of gray smoke as it moves in front of the moon and casts dapple shadows on the midnight sky.

It is life. It is God. What amulet do you possess that will equal the splendor of twilight? What voice are you listening to? Who are your teachers? What can they say to you that the silence doesn't know? You are God. Wake up! You hypocrites; you spiritual entities. There is no such thing. It is a dream. To say, "I want to be spiritual" is really to say, "I am a failure. I am desiring to be spiritual." It means you don't own it.

I AM. I AM. I AM. There is no question.

Let's reason this one out. If you strive to be good, it means you are bad. If you strive to be "the metaphysical entity" who is transcending the wrath of dogma, it means you are the dogma. You will never get out of it and walk in your New Age. It will never come. The future never comes, because you are dreaming the dream of something that awaits in the future, which means it isn't now. Do you see?

There is no New Age. Tomorrow never comes if you're hoping for it, because if you hope, it means you do not own it. You're asleep and you have never lived. Wake up! The sun is shining. The rocks are coming down from the mountain.

Life is the rest of the pie!

Whose voice do you hear in the wilderness? Yours!

I AM. The center of **I AM** is forever and ever and ever. The genteel, humble, daring light of a pure entity lies within; that is what is underneath the dreams—all of them.

You are God, dreaming the dream of man who is limited. And on the pallet of the dreamer, **no** thing evolves. You have not evolved since my day. What of your technical age? I knew it in my day. You look like we looked in my day.

And who gave you your technical knowledge? A daring genius who dreamed a dream and walked into his destiny.

Look at your source of lighting. Your lights no longer burn from whale oil. You have trapped the magic of the unseen—the "electrum". Who thought of that? Not you, but the dreamer who embraced emotionally and walked forward. You are still asleep in your dynamic age. You have not evolved since my day. Your heads have not gotten larger to accommodate more brain activity. They don't need to. You use only a third of your brain!

You're asleep on the pallet.

Wake up! Spring is coming. It is evolving. Wake up! The living organism of your earth is evolving—and you are asleep.

A true God who walks in human form does not bow down at the feet of another, nor does he take counsel in another. A true God is the sparkling light of charisma and genius. A true God is filled with gentility and humble strength and a great mind to know, and lives it impeccably. God who walks in human form.

Be aware, dreamers. There are angels walking outside your window. They are dancing in the rain. A truly enraptured child of God is God. And its knowingness is intact; it is acutely aware of all things. Its instincts are as attuned as those of the salmon. It is never unhappy. It left unhappiness in the dream that belonged in the dream.

Waking up is a joy. The pie is **doing**, creating. And any moment it can be finished, and another dream embraced, and another destiny walked into.

Change is evolution. You know you're going somewhere when your attitude is changing. You know you are waking up. When you wake up, will you know what I have said here and what I have not said.

To manifest and dream of freedom is to change the attitude. Your emotions are real.

The truth lies **within**.

The perception of yesterday is illusion.

Your dreams will manifest fervently, and one day you will simply dream **I AM**, embrace it, and you will be the integral part of your own life.

Does a lily in the field wonder about its draperies, the style of its garments? Do the grasses worry about their food and nourishment? Hardly. They live again and again, over and over, and the seeds of the last life are carried in the wind over hill and dale into a very sweet meadow and a new experience.

You want to be happy. You think money will get you there? Never, because money is someone else's ride!

Desire happiness in your dreams, and that will take care of everything else. If you are a noble, kind, impeccable entity, without the deviousness and the wretchedness of yesterday, the joy will fulfill all things.

You are genius. But most of you are fogged by what you are reading. You don't have the brains. You don't have a strong back and besides, you can think of a million excuses why you couldn't do this—and you can create them, too.

I could say, "Sit down right now and think of all the reasons why you are not a genius," and you would still be sitting there in the morning! And what does that say? It shows you how thick the dream that guards all the others is.

You are lazy, lethargic entities who expect everyone else to do it for you. You will never wake up. You'll never live. You don't like hearing that. It stings. Go back to sleep then.

But you are equipped with everything. Know that. You did not come into this life lacking anything you needed to go all the way.

And what about some of you who think that what would make your life brilliant is another human being to make you feel loved? You want someone to make you feel special. Do you know why you are hungry for a relationship? Do you know why you go through relationship after relationship? Because you're going around and around in a box of frustration, and you think that a relationship is the answer and that if you can find someone who can give you the strokes, then you can feel good about sleeping at night.

That whole business of searching for a relationship is really frustrated genius. When you **wake up** and become the doer and take the rest of the pie, the energy that sits frustrated in your loins shifts and changes, and the pituitary opens up and begins to bloom, and all that energy walks forward into destiny. You're **doing**. You're creating. Don't you know that the energy that sits in what you call the root chakra is raw genius? And your nature is to find someone to **relieve** it! You spill your life on the floor!

Celibacy isn't forced. It is waiting there. It is the bridge that takes you from the dream to reality. When you're celibate, the energy shifts in a natural flow of creativity. You're hunting down relationships to make you feel good about sleeping. When you wake up from the dream you've been living, you may find that you're walking alone to your destiny, because you created it that way for that achievement.

You don't get married when you pass this plane. You don't go strolling in a sack of clouds when you pass. You are pure light energy. God waking up shifts the energy from the human element in you to the creative genius and **becomes** that genius. How? Your dreams; embrace the dreams and wait until they manifest in front of you. Walk into them and meet them. Create. Indulge. Open the brain up, beyond fire, for knowledge. And then, oh, you humans, God will walk in your form.

Requiem for the dream. Requiem for the dream.

The box is your reality and the fantasy is the rest of the pie.

I know there are many of you who have been, shall we say, "put off" by what I've just said. That's because this rattles many boxes, and your boxes represent your way of life. You love to be unhappy and insecure, and the box affords you the security that you need. I have angered many of you with this truth. But if you respond in emotion, I know you have heard it.

There are those of you who are lazy and are motivated only by your loins, by your wombs, and by just getting by. You do want the finer things in life, but if it means you have to make an effort, and if you can get it any other way, you'll take the easy path any day. You are robbers of your own treasure. But there is nothing wrong with that. To stay asleep is all right. You haven't sinned. You are still loved.

Remember this little teaching: The box is your reality and what you call the fantasy is the rest of the pie.

What are the blocks to your path? If you ask that, you don't have a path. Rather than casting your pearls before swine, grasshopper, remember this I have just told you. Write it down if you have to, and put it where you will see it.

If you want to get out of the box, turn it around. Let the box be the illusion and the pie the reality, just in attitude. From the Lord God of Your Being, so be it.

If but one sliver of the pie caused you to smack your lips and make vulgar sounds with your nose and left you wanting, well, that may be the motivation that gets you up off your rear and causes you to walk out and meet your destiny. If you have that motivation, or at least a little sliver of it, you'll continue to taste it.

If your desire is to stay in the box, you don't have a path—just a bed to sleep on.

So if you taste it and you're not jazzed and your motivation wavers, go back to sleep. It's where you want to be.

But I'll make a bargain with those of you who are moving forward. One day when you sit outside the gates, checking everyone out, as it were, and no one passing has anything that you can't own emotionally, you will start to leave no tracks, and I will meet you in the light. So be it.

Now, I recommend that you go and feast now and absorb this new piece of the pie and think about your attitude. Contemplate the possibility of reversing it; for when you can, you can take that attitude beyond death into forever. Then you'll know that all this is real!

After you've added new fuel for the body and new thoughts for the mind, pick this book back up, and we'll see what we can do with another emotional dream.

And if you're one of the ones who's probably going to stay asleep, and you know it, read on anyway. Even in your sleep you'll remember this. By reading and absorbing, even if you don't understand some of it and argue with the rest, you'll get enough pieces to start a process. By working your way through this material, you have gained grand options and truth. You have used pure reason to derive delicious emotional opportunities. You will move mountains. And perhaps, for the first time, you have gotten a flickering of hope about the enigmatic Kingdom of Heaven.

Sure, you've heard for a long time that you're God and that the Kingdom of Heaven lives within you. The reason it's never been a big deal is because those who embraced it aren't here any longer. Only you leftovers are here.

And when you next go to your bed or to your destiny, there will be a quickening of the understanding of an emotional truth that transcends the words.

And when you understand financial freedom, you will have it.

More than you dreamed! Except the difference is, when you come to the hour of your passing, what you have amassed from these dreams will go with you and prepare a mansion for you, in another time and another place, where all things are in harmony together.

So not only will you be able to fulfill all your dreams and leave them behind as a mute legacy of your existence, but you will own them when you leave.

Woe to the rich man who scrambles to hold on and be buried with his jewels, for he goes naked to the light.

Now, go and eat. And when you eat, always bless your food. Bless your bodies. And think about what you have learned emotionally. Think about the buttons that have been pushed, because the impact of the emotion of a truth embraced is yours forever.

*"It is as though a God with a trillion
eyes is awakening from a long nap. And as he
rises, the first thing He sees is Himself. . .
in a mirror. And as you are awakening, so are
many, many others."*

Trick of the Light

You are God Who is Dreaming He is Man

You are birthed from the thought within which all things exist. You are beautiful.

Your skin colors are like a color pallet. Some of you have skin like polished mahogany, a beautiful rich color. Some are yellow, paler even than a daffodil. Some of you are pink, blushing inside. You are beautiful. There isn't any difference in any of you. You're just part of the light and you are exquisitely beautiful.

There are eyes that are every shade of brown and some that are green like reeds, feline and mystical. There are blues in different shades of the sky at different times of the day; they dance, twinkle, and burn with life. Some eyes I have seen are gray, like the water of a clam.

Some of you have hair like polished copper, slate, mellow sun color, ebony. Some are like the snowy white peaks of a mountain. Some of you are drab and dull, and some of you are shining bright and lustrous.

Beautiful bodies. You are homo erectus. Homo sapiens. You come in large, small, broad, wide, flabby, taut, thin, stout. But you all have the same skeletal frame: beautiful.

God who is dreaming He is man.

When I see the intensity of your lights varying, it doesn't mean one of you has more or less light than another, but that you are all different, creative, beautiful; yet I see you the same, as God, though each is unique.

When I look into your eyes and watch your hair, I'm seeing

that which transcends the dream in reality called "magnificent display of human drama, unfolding, waking up, becoming that great light again."

It's when you **become** the Light that you can see it in others. Not one of you is paler than another. You are beautiful. That is that.

How wonderful it will be for you wondrous entities who are searching for freedom when you can look out at the lot of the world and not judge one as less than another. How blissful when you can look at your fellow man and not envy and not be jealous, for that is what has formed those fathomless depths of emptiness within you. When your attitude changes, you see things differently. You no longer are the blind man with your heavy lids thick in matter.

Do you know that when you envy, when you're empty, it's what you don't own that you are feeling? When you own it, peace reigns.

There is no power that walks in the **human** dream, no matter how much money and control is involved; even if the world is the chessboard you play your games on. Those who play that game of money and control walk the human dream where one thing cannot be conquered: that is **love**.

When you love, you step outside the game. But first, before you can render such love, you must be the **king** who **eats** the pie because you know you deserve it, because it's yours. And with that, you can love the whole of the world.

Love. That's one of those words that sort of sounds like "Big deal, nothing new." But have you tried it lately? Hardly!

It's the crust of the pie.

When everyone begins to play their final role in the game, imagine the entities whose method of playing has been all of that money and all of that power. The meek who own the love will be unaffected, because they cannot be manipulated, controlled, or hypnotically induced. Their peace comes from the wellspring of the soul, wherein lies the richness of noble things—of honor, love, impeccability, truth, forgiveness, and gentility of spirit. Do you know how much harm you do to yourself when you judge another? You thicken the dream. Is it really worth that?

In the wellspring you learn to love—so much so that one day, as you sit in the dawning of your morning, a warrior walks up to you and lo, he carries a great broadsword with a hilt ten men can put their hands around, and with blood in his eye, he says to you, "I have come to destroy you," and you will have such love that you can look back into his eye and say, "If it fulfills you, do so."

Now, that may seem very far fetched. How could you possibly sit there and let someone do that? A grand thing occurs when there is no energy given to a thing, just total surrender, not a superficial surrender, but the complete surrender that demands being in a place where you can say, "When you cleave my body into parts, you only free my soul."

There is no energy given. There is no friction. There is no war. There is no anger. There is no regret, no remorse, no judgment.

And the great soldier drops his sword and it clatters to the ground, and it sits there, reflecting blades of light back to the heaven, and he begins to weep because there is no conquest. He doesn't achieve anything. There is no whimpering entity begging for his life. There is only truth. And he sits and cries a thousand days over the mystery.

Eventually, he'll be the man sitting in the road.

Love is part of manifestation.

Love is caring enough about the possibility of the enigma of God being the reality that you switch the attitude to the inward process which gives credence and value to your existence. Faith has nothing to do with it.

When you love yourself enough to wake up from your dreams, from your bondage, or from your dream of being victimized, talked about, ridiculed, and persecuted, it means that you are starting to love who you are.

To love yourself is very selfish. But without that, you cannot love another. It is sheer hypocrisy to be without love for self and to profess it for another. It is hypocrisy to live for another and not for the sake of yourself, for without loving yourself, the love you profess for another becomes brittle and blows away in the wind.

You **learn** to love you. You begin to admire you, to respect your genius and your courage. And you begin to admire the deployment, if you will, of effort and desire. If you can find yourself admirable, honorable to your emotions, so that your words represent your feelings, you'll find that you're an adorable creature! And then remember, you can only see in someone else what you see in yourself.

And that is where love begins. That is what is meant by unconditional love.

Now do you understand that aspect of the process?

If they say they despise you, you can still love them. They can have their truth, and you can still have yours.

It is so rare to find one who knows that the legacy of God is within, and rarer still for that one to **love** the within. And yet the concepts are synonymous, mutually agreeable to one another.

Every manifestation you do, every dream that you relieve yourself of the burden of, takes you closer to love. The very act of engaging in self-possibilities is love. It is the beginning.

Love is not the lust of the loin or the womb. It is not the reflection of painted faces and mirrors. It is not the color of your clothing, your hair, your eyes. You are never satisfied with any of that!

Love is the **within**, what you are, your essence. And the more of your dreams and the more of the pie from which you partake and manifest, the greater you come to love yourself, until that love stretches itself into a broad, all-encompassing knowingness, so that if that warrior cleaved you in two, you could be at peace with him and his word.

Love never dies, Masters. It is elusive to the godless. But with the **living**, it never dies. It is continuous. Continuous. I know that what seems normal is an illusion. It is normal to envy. It is normal to be malicious. It is normal to be wicked and fallible.

*Masters, **normal** is the drug that keeps you asleep!*

Don't you know that the great abnormal don't walk this plane any longer?

I listen to you talk. I see you struggle to try to match the words with the emotion inside of you, trying to be truthful through and through. I see many of you take it earnestly. And there are others of you who chew their lips and reveal white, shining, carnivorous teeth, and you have to bite your tongue to keep from being normal!

It should roll smoothly, like the morning mist.

"From the Lord God of My Being, I call forth the Father this day into all that is life, to all that is genius, to all that is me."

And in the same breath that speaks those words, you issue forth the love and all its possibilities. It is magic! It's the crust of the pie. Wondrous things will come with this knowledge. Immense freedom will come in many areas, and many of you will go to the wind, forever and ever. But you have to cherish what you are enough to think that you are worth it.

You have to love the dream enough to give birth to it, which means that you **must love** the Creator. No one out there, outside the window, close to where you slumber, is worth giving it all away for, because it seems **normal**. I see you in all that you are, in all the shades that you are, and in the different stages of the sleep. And I love you completely, for I have found that you are worth it, because I have been you and I have dreamed the dream and awakened from it, much to the dismay of many around me!

The faceless few who control your economy, your market that's called stock, your revolutions, and your laws which enslave you, the men who wish to own all the kings and all the king's men, do not own nature. It is the greatest rebel of all. Man cannot harness it, because it is evolving.

When you go through this process, dream after dream, getting yourself **fixed** in your needs, make sure that when you move outside the box, you leave the door open for possibilities. Do it in a quantum of understanding and love, so that through the flow of that love, in the natural process of evolution, you stay in alignment with nature.

What is nature? It is God, for heaven's sake. If you stay in alignment with nature in this process, you will be outside that which ensnares, that which blinds and binds, and you will have that great freedom you desire.

And you should **see** that before you pass this plane. You should see all of that before you slip beyond the gate and watch. You should know that impeccable knowledge with which you are aligned, for it is vital, rich, fiery, moving, and untamable. **Life.** Then the game will not affect you.

Make no mistake. You won't be able to sit in the boughs of a great tree and do nothing. You will have to be on the move with your destiny, walking with it, marching with it, and acutely aware of instinct. You will have to be in knowingness and in emotion.

Now, a word for those of you who let yourselves get just a little near the front door, just to the door handle. And you listen. You don't hear anything out there. No galloping horseman. No wind. Nothing. And you start to get a little afraid. So you turn up the stereo, and the noise makes you feel better. So you go back to the door, and you just know you forgot something. "What was it?" But, of course, the **past**. "I can't possibly go until I pack all of my troubles."

Be very, very, very careful about your troubles, the way you pack them. No wrinkles. They take priority over everything else. Well, your past is important to you!

But when you pack all your bags and go back to the door, you realize that there are too many of them. You can't possibly get beyond that door unless you have it all with you, but you can't get through the door with it.

Leaving Yesterday Behind

So you sit there and think about it.

"I can't leave this behind. I have invested all my life in this. What will people think about me, if? If? If? If?

"What am I going to say to them now that I don't hurt any longer? I kept it up for a long time. It paid off big!

"And what are people going to think about me when I'm sort of giddy and happy and outrageous? I've got to have something that is sort of **real** to me.

"And for God's sake, what about all those past lives! I don't have nearly enough bags for all that! Not to mention, of course, the trunks I'll need for everything everyone has ever said about me.

"Why, I wouldn't even exist without some supportive evidence."

The past is what you linger in, in your dream. It's what keeps you in a box. You can't change your past. There will only be a now. And you are afraid to give it up, afraid to be loving and compassionate. You are afraid to have a new day, beaming with health, with no more problems.

Many people never make it out the door because they've overburdened themselves.

How does this fit with your first manifestation?

Why is it that you have to go out and buy a new hat to make you happy? Yet it only takes wearing it once to get tired of it. How many of them must you have to realize that you are just not happy?

This manifestation of the first dream that you embraced is working collectively as a destiny in front of you. What happens when you go to see it in front of you and realize that you have to open the door to meet it? You know it's out there. You can't hear it, but you know it's there. And you can't get beyond that door because you can't forget yesterday.

In other words, you can't forgive yourself, not for yesterday, but for living in it. So what happens to the manifestation? Well, it's outside the door.

Now, along comes an entity who is just itching to find something to do, and he is walking straight ahead. You know, he's not one of those puny spiritual people. He's a doer. He bumps right into the outside of the door and here's this manifestation just sitting there. It's just like a rosy, red apple just waiting to be plucked from the tree. And, of course, he plucks it. "It's mine." And he runs out and patents it! You read about it in the paper that you get through the little slit in the door!

You sit there and your head is pounding in this dream. And there is a gnashing of teeth and there is cursing, turning the inside of your box all blue. And there is spite and remorse and hate and bitterness. And you just **know** the sucker stole it from you.

Let me tell you what happens. That destiny is created by you. Where do you think new ideas come from? Bright ideas come from someone far away who emotionally created them. The bright idea wasn't necessarily created by the holder, but it was picked up by the searcher. It looms out there. It is ready for someone to come along who is looking for it. They pick it from the tree. They pick up the idea from consciousness, because they are looking for it. That's what they want. That's **their** dream.

You see, you created it, but you couldn't get beyond the safety of your own yesterdays. You couldn't get beyond the comfort zone of your own miseries, hang-ups, dogmas, and all of that, to even get to your own manifestation.

So who is the genius? Well, you read in the paper, of course, that they are acknowledging that this man who plucked your manifestation from the ethers is a genius, that he made a remarkable contribution to mankind. His stock has soared on the market, and he is picking his teeth, pushing himself away from the pie!

Bright ideas come from an emotional being somewhere who emotionally embraced their concept, went out, and **became** them in consciousness. The one searching for a bright idea in his dream gets it. He doesn't create it. He just **gets** the idea. His emotion is picking his teeth. You see? Patting his stomach. I tell you this because when we talk of genius and we talk of one who can't get beyond the door, we are talking of one who has no love for himself, of one who has learned to be somewhat emotional, but has no follow-through. And every dream that you embrace which was the limitation that hung **here, will** happen. But you have to get up and go get it. You have to go through the door. And if it means leaving yesterday behind, it is necessary to do so.

Don't you know that a Christ has no past? It is only the Christ.

It is a characteristic neither of evolution nor of nature to look back and sigh over old bones! Man tries to preserve them. Where's your state of mind residing? Nature doesn't care. It goes forward. Nature operates on the same truth I am teaching you.

There is great genius out there, because there are great dreams waiting to be embraced. But there is also much laziness out there.

You can't get beyond the door without packing too many bags of yesterday. And really, the bags are just an excuse not to go through the door. Whether you go on to all of the pie or not, you did make a contribution to someone out there when you embraced your first dream. It has your name all over it. You are its creator.

But if you do not claim it, someone else will. All great ideas come from the emotional creator who dreamed them.

How many stories have you heard of someone who said, "Yeah, I thought of that years ago." Hmmm. Made you scratch your head and ask, "Really?" You wondered why, if he had the idea, he didn't do something with it.

Your dreams are the same and so is your freedom. It is follow-through. Catch my drift?

Let me repeat what I said about genius, because I know some of you fogged out.

Genius is the ability to dream a dream and then do something with it.

The very walking forward opens up the emotional body that allows the emotional mind to open, which is your brain, and, in turn, thought and action follow. Action and reaction. The one dream that is realized, manifested, and **owned** is called genius. And, in turn, your consciousness opens up for more, and the energy begins to feed you.

Hear you of a Master da Vinci? He was a genius, right? Everything he emotionally embraced, he put into script.

Now, he is called a genius. But he really is a dreamer, because it wouldn't be until much, much later in your time flow that what he drew became someone else's bright idea. He was ahead of himself in time. But really, he stayed in a box. Do you understand? What if da Vinci went forward and created what he conceived? Why didn't he go a little further in working with his underwater concepts? He could have.

How different would your world have been if da Vinci had walked through the door in front of him and embraced every one of his dreams? Quite different, dear people. Quite different. But instead, his greatest attribute is a forlorn, drab woman. He painted himself and how he was—just a drab, half-smiling dreamer.

Point made?

What does it take? What makes the difference?

Love. It takes love. That's what gives you the guts to walk through the door. It is love that opens the door. It is love that leaves the bags behind. It is love that sees things as opportunities. And it is love that takes you out of the drugged state of being asleep.

If you **feel**, then you have learned, because there is one thing that you don't do in the dream. In the dream, you don't forget anything emotional. That's what your dead weight is all about. Get it?

There is a very frustrating thing I tell my daughter when she is in the murk and the mire of all things. I tell her there is no such thing as a problem. It doesn't exist unless you want it there. And, of course, if you can create it, the answer lies in the problem.

There is nothing that you can create that you can't uncreate. Nothing. Even nothing you can uncreate.

If you own all of this emotionally, great are your days that are coming, for you will find them joyful, not fearful.

*"Learn to see. When you can truly see, you
will find yourself looking directly into the
eye of God. And if you get frustrated, you can
always do what you did with me," said Chris,
his lips bending into a sly grin.
"What's that?"
"Get fed up with searching and **decide** to find.
You see, many of those stuck in the illusion have
sentimentally glorified the search for Truth;
they have become more attached to **looking** for
Truth than to finding the Truth. Ironically,
they've boxed themselves into such a corner that
they can't even accept directions from someone
who's actually arrived at the destination."*

Trick of the Light

There Are No Words

To endeavor to put into speech this teaching about God, about feelings, and about manifestation, to communicate with sensitive entities who only hear because they are intellectual, is very arduous.

You have never understood God, because you didn't know how to feel. And in the past, you have taken my words, memorized them, carved them up, and tasted them, until they became an intellectualized truth.

You distilled them down to just "You are God."

And you have used that truth to excuse your bad behavior and your duality.

It served its purpose.

But to communicate what is **within, that** is pure power, absolute power. It stands still in its own time.

*There is no **time** when you go within and embrace emotion. It just is. It's the **IS**. I have not words for this.*

Nobody has really **heard** this up until now. They couldn't understand.

Feel? What is that?

They say, "But I love you, Ram."

And so I tell them that I am worth loving. Why? Because, if they could find compassion with me, it meant that they were still alive. I have stayed to find the magic that would turn it around and send it back to you a thousandfold, so that what you have felt for me, you could begin to feel inside **you**.

And so I sent runners and then more words, and you would cut and paste them according to your ability to hear.

But in utilizing this process, in tapping your own emotion and unleashing your own power, you are finding your own truth.

Don't you know those are the words I could never find?

It takes **your** words to find **your** truth.

And if you have gained that from this information, then thank God. Hold onto it forever and let no thing cleave it from you. You **will** see God in this lifetime. So be it.

Embracing the Dream of God.

Now. It is time to do a biggie.

I desire for you to embrace and to manifest through emotion.

I desire for you to create a drama—a high drama. And at the moment that you go into the **within**, to create that drama, I want you to be aware that you are feeling the dream of God.

In other words, embrace emotionally and powerfully so that everything that you are embracing emotionally is the **living truth**. Get it?

Let me say this again, another way. Embrace and create a drama, a fantasy, a beauteous, wild, delicious picture that gives you whatever it is you want as if you had a Midas touch—except, make that a **magic** touch.

In this process, I want you to live and contemplate everything that you are desiring and see it occurring **in the moment**. It is like this that all is made possible!

*We are dealing with the dream that is holding everything else back here. It is called **attitude**.*

Your current picture says, "**This** is real. **That** is fantasy."

What this dream will do, if you own it, is turn that around. So you will say, "I see. **That** is real. And **this** is fantasy. I had it backwards all this time!"

The Process: Physical Directions

Get comfortable. Sit on the earth or on the floor. Loosen your clothing. Take responsibility for your life.

If you are doing this process in a group for demonstration purposes, this time if your neighbor rolls on the floor, roll with him. If he is laughing, laugh with him—not at him, but **with** him. If she is tickling your fantasy and she triggers a wonderful spilling over of cheerful mirth, let it roll.

That is emotion! It is joyful! It is sweet and refreshing, and it quickens your dream.

Remember, you are all brothers unto one another. You are connected through the mind of God.

Be at peace with everyone around you. When you can feel that connectedness, you'll walk in peace.

Get ready.

Remove all your adornments.

Remember, your metals carry the frequency of yesterday.

To bring the alignment into **now**, your body should be naked of metal.

And for those of you who have a mouthful, you are forgiven!

Unloosen your girth.

Remove your shoes.

Do not begin this process until you find yourself comforted. If you are in a group and you cannot find your comfort in that setting, just listen and learn from those around you. You can do this alone when you are home without a demonstration from anyone.

Breathe.

Close your eyes.

Manifestation prayer

FROM THE LORD GOD OF MY BEING
UNTO THE FATHER WITHIN
UNTO THAT WHICH IS YOU,
I NOW JOURNEY.
OPEN UP,
FOR COME I HOME.
UNTO THIS HOUR,
BRING FORTH
THE POWER,
THE KNOWINGNESS,
THE MANIFESTATION.
FROM THE LORD GOD OF MY BEING
UNTO THE FATHER WITHIN
IT IS LAW.
SO BE IT!

Give thanks to the Father within you for that which is truth, for that which is real, for that which is timeless. For unto God, all things are possible. Giving thanks to that gives recognition to the Lord God of Your Being, Unto You, whatever be your name.

"Remember to see, and not just look
For nothing is as it seems
This alley is a road into the sky
And you but another dream."
Trick of the Light

May Your Wishes Come to Pass

Yeshua Ben Joseph said, in attempting the forty days in the wilderness, "Get behind me, Satan." He was addressing his alter ego. In that process in the desert, he embraced all the cities of the world. He owned them, one by one. When he finished one, he went on to the next, and the next. He pulled away from the languor of them, and when he was done, he came out thirsty and hungry, and he went straight to a wedding.

The truth is, the Miracle Man got that way by eliminating all his dreams. And what are dreams? Suppressed temptations! And he did it with no less vigor and drama and sincere emotion than you should be using now.

I wish you to know that in my lifetime I sat upon a rock for seven years in contemplation of the world around me. When the wind teased me upon my face and blew my cloak all around my competent being, I had to own it. I had to. It took me many years to figure out how to be that once again. It wasn't until then that I became the wind in all that I perceived within my being the wind to be: wild and free, powerful, blowing up, revealing young knees, causing laughter in children, turning emerald leaves to silver, and pushing the stagnation off the pond.

I was the wind underneath the great wings of wild fowl.

And through that same drama of becoming, I so extended my consciousness that my mind bent in two in **becoming** that.

There was no turning back, for there was no alternative.

The law was in force.

You do not have to do anything any different than any great Master has done. And, by the way, many have remained great Masters. Very few have gone on to be the Christ in greater frontiers, greater realities. Some have remained just magicians. That's all.

So with your vigor, your enthusiasm, and your pressing desire to be a part, you have created a unique consciousness.

It is called your reality.

And truly, if only you throw open the door and meet your destiny, one day you will become as I have become.

And all who have warranted your utmost respect and love, you will meet again.

But you have to walk out to meet them.

Never be ashamed of your emotions.

Never be ashamed of your joy.

And never, never be ashamed of your tears that so sweetly reveal limitation. Be thankful for them.

Thank God you are alive.

You are **feeling** intelligence.

So where does all this come back to financial freedom? Through knowledge. Just simple knowledge. You have learned about gold and paper dollars. The **Graymen** own it. You don't.

Through this understanding, you will walk, through pure reasoning, out of a narrow-minded vision and into an unlimited sphere.

Desire what you want. Live it. Be it. Taste it. Smell it. It is. And it will be!

Never desire to have money so that you can have time for God. With all your Mind and all your Being, desire to be God. The rest is incidental.

Be kind to yourself. If you are eager to run out and invest in something that will make you a fortune overnight, invest in you by giving yourself the time to recapture these precious moments.

Give yourself time to be emotional, to live the dream, to eat the pie. It is yours. **See** the manifestation come into being.

Walk forward into your destiny. Own it—dream after dream after dream.

And one day, entity, there won't be anything else to own, for you will **be** everything. That is the secret of every entity that ever **became** God who woke up dreaming about man.

I will give you a blessing for this process of manifestation and the desire you have exhibited to **know** and to **feel**.

From the Lord God of My Being, to all that have yelled out, to all that have proclaimed, to all that have laughed in rolling thunder. From the Father within me, to the Father within to which all things respond, may your wishes come to pass to the glory of God the Father, and all eternity, and all time to come.

And may you be the light that reveals the shadows of the world.

I will be with you in your days to come! And to those of you on the path, you'll find there aren't really any blocks. As you grow hungry for more knowledge, I'll be here. In the wind. And in the thought. And in the fantasy.

Other Books About Ramtha

I Am Ramtha
The first high-quality, full-color photographic and text book on a channeled entity and his teachings. *$24.95 hardcover.*

Ramtha
A beautifully edited and designed collection of the cornerstones of Ramtha's teachings. *$19.95 hardcover.*

A State of Mind, My Story: Ramtha, The Adventure Begins
JZ Knight's moving autobiography in which she tells the story of her life and her involvement with Ramtha. *$15.95 hardcover.*

Becoming, A Masters Manual
Edited by Khit Harding, this book provides a collection of quotes from Ramtha's teachings. *$14.95 quality paperback.*

Destination Freedom: A Time-Travel Adventure
Douglas James Mahr's wonderfully inspiring adventure, under Ramtha's guidance, exploring self-discovery. *$10.95 quality paperback.*

Ramtha Intensive: Soulmates
Transcribed from Ramtha's January 1986 audience on soulmates, love, and relationships. *$10.00 quality paperback.*

Ramtha Intensive: Change, The Days To Come
Transcribed from Ramtha's May 1986 audience on man, the environment, and what nature has in store. *$10.00 quality paperback.*

Voyage To The New World
A collection of Ramtha's teachings and commentaries written by Douglas James Mahr. *$9.95 quality paperback.*

Manifesting, A Masters Manual
A collection of Ramtha quotes, edited by Khit Harding, to help your understanding of self. *$7.95 quality paperback.*

Last Waltz of the Tyrants
Reveals the extraordinary challenges and opportunities facing mankind in the days to come. *$7.95 quality paperback.*

UFOs and the Nature of Reality
Understanding alien consciousness and interdimensional mind. *$11.00 quality paperback.*

Other Beyond Words Titles

Trick of the Light
A book of transformation and discovery. $9.95 *quality paperback.*

Other Resource Materials

To experience Ramtha in person, or on audio or video tapes, contact Ramtha Dialogues, P.O. Box 1210, Yelm, WA 98597, or call 206-458-5201.

Windwords: The First Two Years
Combines all of the 1986 and 1987 Windwords newspaper issues. 206-446-7799 or 1-800-223-8106, P.O. Box 576-S, Rainier, WA 98576. *$19.95 quality paperback.*

Publisher's Note

Beyond Words Publishing, Inc., produces books of uncompromising standards and integrity, books that invite us to step beyond the limits of our experience to discover what lies within, beyond words.

Our publications include children's, photographic, nature, self-help, New Age and psychology books, as well as calendars and audio tapes.

For a free catalog of our newest titles, please contact:

Beyond Words Publishing, Inc.
Pumpkin Ridge Road
Route 3, Box 492-B
Hillsboro, OR 97123
503-647-5109
1-800-284-9673

A celebration of life through publishing.